grow
and
gather

A GARDENER'S GUIDE TO
A YEAR OF CUT FLOWERS

GRACE ALEXANDER

photography by Dean Hearne
illustrated by Rob Mackenzie

Hardie Grant

QUADRILLE

contents

I.
INTRODUCTION

Gardening is an inherently paradoxical activity. It means existing at the point of tension between being and doing, between accepting the majesty and might of nature, and striving to imprint a human hand upon the earth. To plant a seed is to hope and to invest, but to avoid going entirely mad, this has to be done with an acknowledgement of the fact there are no guarantees. And that we can only do so much. The movement of a garden sets it aside from other art forms; no stasis is ever reached, there is no 'finished'. There is always weeding to be done or a border to be addressed. There will always be chard running to seed and a hedge threatening to claim its birthright as a row of trees.

To grow and to garden is a radical act of rebellion. To rest, to rest in a garden, to drink in its beauty and its complexity and its imperfection and to just be – this is where true revolution lies. And this book is a call to arms. By all means do, but promise me that you will also just be. Notice. Acknowledge. Know the sensuality of a garden that is truly loved.

I'm not sure which came first for me, psychology or gardening. I spent my childhood in the gardens of Wisley and Arley Hall, Hidcote and Dunham Massey. I dabbled with landscape design at school, and moved a vegetable garden plant by plant when we sold our family farm when I was 15. Then I became a psychologist, but the growing was always there.

I work in child protection, and when people discover what I do they all see it the same way. What an antidote, they say. How wonderful to have such pleasure. Gardening is therapy, they say.

But I do not find it so and I don't think I have ever found it so. I can be in my field and be overwhelmed by the potential, the work, the creeping chaos of the weeds and the responsibility of conjuring up beauty from the earth on which I stand. Deciding where to put paths and perennials can feel like an unbearable level of commitment. Planting out fragile seedlings can seem like subjecting them to intolerable vulnerability. When the slugs ate the heads off my narcissi, I felt it like a pain that made me catch my breath.

For years, I didn't know why I did it. Gardening is not an addiction, more a compulsion. It is not an antidote to my work, but a mirror. I inhabit two worlds, with different rules, and clothes, and languages and imperatives. Whatever commonalities there are between them have to be found within me. Gardening is a way of distilling my essence. A way of knowing myself though a relationship with the ground.

I am not impatient but I am impulsive. I buy many more seeds than I could ever grow and I have killed more plants than I care to name by purchasing them and never putting them in the ground. I rush from thing to thing, with passion and enthusiasm but little forward thinking. I vastly underestimate how long things will take and try to pack too much in. The sun often sets long before I have got through my to-do list. Seedlings languish in seed trays because I am at work, or because I can't decide where to put them.

But I am loyal to the end. I express my gratitude frequently and openly. Me and my field are a team and, while I don't always get it right, my intentions are good and I tend her with love. When I am there I am there with all my heart, and the root of all my enthusiasm and big ideas is passion. Passion for beauty and creativity and the magic that is the process of a seed becoming a plant and a flower. The art and the science of combining texture and colours to produce something so much greater than the sum of their parts.

I do not garden because it is therapeutic. It challenges me and it finds my edges. I do it because I am compelled to increase the amount of beauty in the world. I garden because I cannot not.

This book is an effort to take the passion and courage and enthusiasm that I have, and to curb my inability to appreciate what simply is. Through writing it, I have taken the time to document, to notice, to narrate a year of my field in flower. It is a blend of planning and wonder, of moments of intensity, reflection and awareness in my garden, structured in a way that even I can manage to keep up with. It opens up the process of growing on every scale.

Each chapter takes you through the tasks and the highlights of the season. There are practical how-tos, and explanations, and my own recommendations and flower and plant favourites. There is also a list of all the mistakes I have ever made growing flowers, so you don't have to make them too. That said, if a season passes and you have done nothing practical but simply watched the spring shoots grow or the autumn leaves fall, this book celebrates that as a worthy and valuable pastime, too.

No getting overwhelmed, no paralysis or discouragement.

Just the creation and allowance of beauty.

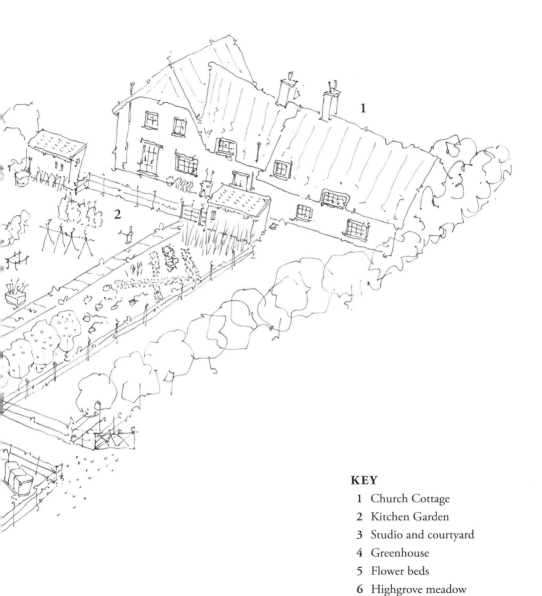

KEY

1 Church Cottage
2 Kitchen Garden
3 Studio and courtyard
4 Greenhouse
5 Flower beds
6 Highgrove meadow
7 Peony bed
8 Espalier apple trees
9 Stone fruit orchard
10 The allotment
11 Fete field

my field

Ten years ago, my flower field was just a sheep field. For some obscure planning reasons, a little section was fenced off by the local estate from the expanse that separated a little row of thatched cottages and the East Deane way as it passes along the bottom of Pickeridge Hill, where Somerset very nearly becomes Devon. It was filled with trees, field maples and the like. Someone put goats in there and they ate the trees. Before I lived here, my neighbour's daughter rode over for Sunday lunch each week and so the field was fenced so they could turn out the horse for a few hours. The neighbour moved and a variety of sheep and lawnmowers did battle with the thistles, nettles and tufty grasses for a number of years, until we found each other.

We bought the middle one of those thatched cottages in 2010 and were persuaded to also take on responsibility for the problematic quarter of an acre that sits at the end of the back garden. I pretended to be reluctant.

An entirely blank, square canvas. At least it was once we had dug out the remaining, struggling trees. And then I planted apple maiden whips, and made long, no-dig beds, and sowed many, many seeds...

THE ORCHARD

A line was drawn down the centre of the square, and a row of apple trees was planted along it for espaliering: a mix of eaters, cookers and traditional cider varieties, selected for their names. Some simply because I liked them: Beauty of Bath and Kingston Black. Some for our nephews' names: William Crump, James Grieve, Tom Putt. We also added a grid of stone fruit and the odd pear tree. Plus a quince, even though the field is a little too dry for it to thrive. And because my weakness for flowers was strong even then, a great white cherry (*Prunus* 'Tai Haku') and an autumn-flowering cherry.

Over the years the trees have grown and fruited and we have added a wood-fired pizza oven, a long trestle table and eventually, when all the hard work was done, a hammock.

THE FLOWER FIELD

The south-facing half of the field was a cutting garden. All flowers. Beds
and beds of David Austin roses. Swathes of nigella. A spine of woven hazel
rods down the central alley. A meadow. The odd raspberry planted many
years ago that pops up with boring regularity in unexpected places. A formal
box-edged bed for structure by the narrow wicket gate. A hedge of *Viburnum
tinus* and lilacs for cutting. The majority of the space is now taken up by
matrix planting, a tapestry of sculptural spires, annual and perennial flowers,
and an underplanting of grasses.

Matrix planting is a type of planting design drawing on the theory of a good
fruitcake: stoic and solid 'background' plants, such as grasses and leafy plants,
form soft swathes in which the feature plants can be studded, like raisins.
I like cherries and almonds in my fruitcake, so my matrix planting has some
seriously big hitters (*Stipa gigantea*, *Helianthus* 'Lemon Queen') to make
it truly memorable. All the plants were chosen for me by Joshua Sparkes
(Head Gardener at Forde Abbey, and expert in all things soil) to be
also good for both cutting and growing from seed.

As a seed merchant, the flowers I grow now are the ones I provide the seed
for. For experimenting and testing – that is what I tell myself. Although this
does not explain why I still have about 50 peonies and rows and rows of
dahlias. None of these are grown from seed.

THE ALLOTMENT

A new addition. Here are all the flowers for dyeing textiles: woad, rows
of black scabious, marigolds and *Coreopsis tinctoria*, all in a chestnut-paling
allotment-style area. The paling fence provides extra protection from the
rabbits (and the Irish setters who live with me) and a containing boundary
for an exploding area of colour and beauty.

THE KITCHEN GARDEN

This was the back lawn. A stretch of grass between the courtyard and the back gate. I started with a few raised beds, and then a few more, and then all the grass went and the whole area, from edge to edge, was turned over to vegetables. A diamond kitchen garden mirroring the lead on the old cottage windows was designed by Kristy Ramage, and I have filled the spaces with chard and leeks and kohlrabi. A rusted metal fence divides off the dedicated squash and pumpkin patch, overhung by next door's huge Bramley apple tree.

morag, maud and hugo

I now have not a dog, but dogs. Three. Three big dogs, that take up the sofa, and would take up the bed if I let them. Joyful, happy, beautiful dogs.

Two of them are particularly beautiful. Morag and Maud are aunt and niece. They are Irish setters, tall, elegant and copper coloured. They look almost identical and it takes a trained eye to tell them apart. However, they are chalk and cheese in terms of morality.

Morag is a good girl. Although she didn't come to live with us until she was over a year old, I met her as a puppy and she was angelic even then. There is simply not a bad bone in her body. All she asks is an armchair to call her own and a good run out in the early evening. She is enthusiastic in her greetings, her tail wagging so wide that her body almost bends in half. In the mornings, when the door to the kitchen is opened, she rushes upstairs like a hare out of the traps, desperate to say good morning, and then go to sleep on the blankets. She only really has two settings: asleep and running.

Maud's mornings look very different. She is slow to wake, and even slower to get out of bed. She adores a lie in and she needs a very good reason to leave the warmth of the kitchen. Maud is all about late nights and hell-raising. When people ask which is which, I tell them to look at what they are doing. If the dog is being good, it is Morag. If it is being mischievous and reckless, it is Maud. Maud digs holes in the orchard, and chases imaginary rabbits through the dahlias. She stares, stock still, into the hedgerows for pigeons. She is never happier than when there is a party; she loves people, but she also lives for champagne corks. She can hear a pop from three rooms away and will come running. We excuse her behaviour by blaming her youth; she came to us when she was nine months old and looked so young that we referred to her as Puppers. Although she is now four years old, she is called Maud only rarely – mostly because if you are calling for a disobedient dog named 'Puppers' in public, people are more likely to judge your dog training leniently.

Morag and Maud »

The girls are cared for by Hugo. As a cocker spaniel, Hugo believes he is in charge of everyone and everything. The girls find his efforts to organize them hilarious and tend to bat him on the head with their paws when he gets above himself. He tries hard, though, and washes their faces and shouts at anyone who might wish to do them harm. I think deep down, Hugo thinks he is a person and he certainly takes the gardening more seriously than the setters. The girls take one look at the outdoors and if it doesn't involve a walk or a picnic, will immediately retreat to the sofa. Huge devotedly follows me up and down the paths, traipsing behind the wheelbarrow or making nests in the hedgerow to watch me weed. He doesn't want to leave me alone, but it is quite clear that he'd rather we were all sitting down indoors having a cup of tea. Hugo is an elegant sort of chap, and enjoys nothing more than sitting upright on his chair at the dinner table, observing the conversation. That, or lying on his back with his feet in the air asking for his tummy to be tickled.

II.
SPRING:
REBIRTH & REGENERATION

MARCH

THE GARDEN JOURNAL

I started keeping a daily garden journal two years ago. It began as a practical record of what was sown when, harvest times for roses and raspberries, first and last frost dates in this uniquely sheltered valley. All those things that gardeners need to jot down because you think you'll remember but you never do. The act of taking the time to not only witness but also document and share the magical goings on in the flower field has deepened my appreciation and delight in the wonders of growing.

TUESDAY 3

Spring. Finally it is spring. I spy the white of the buds on the honesty. There are violets in the grass. On the bank at the top of the lane there is a patch of black widow irises. The turn of the month seems to mark the start of something new. No change in the rain though.

THURSDAY 5

A dinner from the kitchen garden. The purple sprouting broccoli has not been prolific but it is delicious. Supplemented by the immortal chard and the first pickings from a flourishing bed of Russian red kale.

SATURDAY 7

I stop and watch bumblebees. I take delight because of the noticing. Setters do not need to do this; they delight in everything. Especially things they are not meant to be doing, such as digging holes and chasing the scent of rabbits across the tulip beds.

SUNDAY 8

By the time night falls, I hear a storm coming and I go out to check the greenhouse door is secure. Greenhouses look so eerie in moonlight; they glow silver. As I turn back to the house, I catch the comforting smell of woodsmoke.

THURSDAY 12

Nature, in its indifference and its power, is turning towards spring. The woods and the stream banks are a solid, glossy green of wild garlic. The blossom is starting on the old wood of the blackthorn, not just the fresh tips. The bullace, a wild plum, that entwines with an old holly tree is showing signs of life. The furry buds of the goat willow glitter softly. We walk slowly; breathing the air, holding the silence, noticing the changes.

There are things that are unchanged too. Hugo resembles a pint of Guinness every time he steps out for a walk, black mud up his legs and sides, only his back and the top of his head still white. The big cherry tree in the top corner of the first field is not yet out. The blankets remain on our bed because the nights are still chilly. There is talk of frost tomorrow night. But I invest in the future. I sow tomatoes this week, and leeks. Kale and sweet peas. Scabious. Nigella. Ammi. I sow seeds that will grow to be harvested in the late weeks of summer, which feels like a distant world away right now.

understanding your soil

I f you want to understand growth at the most primitive level, look at your
soil. Get to know her. Know her like the growing partner she is. Some soils
are slow to warm up, some are kind and generous, some mean and frugal.
She may be thirsty, tired, depleted, burnt out. She might be waterlogged,
overfed, sluggish. But whatever her state, if you want to take from her, you
have to give. And it has to be what she needs, not what you find the easiest.

Many proper gardeners and flower growers get their soil tested before they
start. Vials of soil are analyzed for deficiencies and deficits, chemical remedies
suggested and prescribed. I admit that I didn't. My soil is not a complex
creature: I knew her history, her location, and she wears her heart on her
sleeve. Getting to know your soil is not difficult, even if you have never had
mud under your nails before. You just need to use your senses. Fertile soil
smells rich, and touching it will give you a spark of joy and a thrill as if it
were alive. And if you think you can't read with your senses, remember that
your ancestors had no choice but to grow things, that our species is made up
of farmers as well as hunter gatherers. Having a relationship with the ground
upon which you stand is in your soul.

It was only when I saw the soilscape of my field on a map that the light
dawned. Of course my field is slightly acid loamy soil on top of clay. It
makes perfect sense for it to be. Why? Because if I look to my right I can
see the craggy hills of the Blackdowns rising up. Although the other end of
these hills are peaty and thin soiled, hinting at the nearby heath landscapes
of Exmoor and Dartmoor, the end closest to me is heavy, hard-to-work clay,
with lumps of blue lias stone. The trees, mostly beech, grow thickly and
enthusiastically and the banks that define the drovers' paths remain sturdy
and strong. Arable fields are absent, this is hard land to farm.

My field is where the Blackdowns tumble down and meet the Taunton Vale, a stretch of flat ground that rises up again at the Quantocks on the other side of town, but also sweeps up to the Somerset Levels to the north-east. I heard that the Levels were once called the land of the summers, because in autumn and winter they are so wet as to be uninhabitable. When the rain comes, acres and acres of the area sit underwater, seasonal lakes, visible for miles around. The River Tone regularly breaks its banks and reclaims the road. The trees are not beeches there, but willows.

Situated in between these contrasting landscapes, my soil has a bed of clay, but a layer of beautiful loam on top. The floodplain has been generous once upon a time and tempered the clay with deposits of silt. Under stress and duress, it will revert to slippery sticky clay, but if cared for, it is absolutely perfect. A seam of safety and fertility. In soil terms, it is priceless.

Look down:
» Is your soil heavy or light?
» Free-draining or wet?
» Sloping or flat?

Look up:
» Where is the light?
» The prevailing wind?
» The cold pockets and the sun traps?

Look around:
» What grows well for you and your neighbours?
» What wild weeds thrive around you?

GETTING THE MOST OUT OF YOUR SOIL

Holding your soil in your hands will tell you a lot about its state of health and its character. You will be able to feel how it warms up, how it takes on the heat of your hands, how it clumps or crumbles. Truly sandy soil will trickle through your fingers. Clay you can pick up in clumps. Most soil is, like mine, somewhere in between. Light, crumbly, dark in colour (which means that it has a high level of organic matter) is perfect.

If you have clay soil…

Do not work in wet weather, make paths and stick to them (less important if you do not dig your soil). Add as much compost and organic matter as you can (see page 52). It may be slow to warm up in spring, so pay attention to the soil, not what other people are doing. Do not top-dress if the soil is very cold. Hydrangeas and roses do wonderfully on clay.

If you have sandy soil…

Sandy soil is much lighter than clay, and does not have that annoying tendency to stick to your boots. Holes are easier to dig, and hoes run through it like silk. The downside is that water runs straight through it, so it becomes dusty and dry in even the briefest hot spell, and it is hard to keep nutrients in the soil for the plants. Go for hot, Mediterranean plants that thrive on poor soil: verbenas, lavenders… Bulbs are good because they hold a lot of their own nutrition and won't rot in damp soil over a cold wet winter.

As with clay, the solution is to add as much compost and organic matter as you can. But improving sandy soil can be an uphill struggle, so pick your battles. Many more plants that are tolerant of drought conditions are now available; these will flourish where others struggle.

planning your garden

It is a Sunday afternoon in the earliest days of spring. There is a storm
outside and the rain is hitting the windows horizontally. I have checked
the greenhouse is still standing three times so far today, but that is the only
venturing outside I am going to do. There is a slow-roasting pork shoulder
in the bottom oven. I have a big sheet of paper, and I am going to plan.

First, what do you love? You can grow memories, or scent, or drama,
or subtle, intricate beauty. Do you want everlasting flowers for drying?
To feed the birds and the butterflies and the bees? To make botanical
inks? You can magic up fat dahlias and chocolate foxgloves and towering
sparkling, spangling grasses from the tiniest of seeds. You can have meadows
of wild, tangled confectionery colours, or rows of colour for filling the house
with brightness. You can have tapestries woven from grasses and spires of
perennials and an understory of annuals. If you have the space, you can
have them all.

All you need is some seed and a plan.

In many ways, the process of planning a cutting garden is similar to that of planning a border; it is just the scale and the planting out that is different. Cutting gardens traditionally put all the plants together in rows: a block of cosmos, a row of wigwams of sweet peas, a dahlia bed, a cluster of antirrhinums. They are meant to be hidden round the back, out of view, so that when they are stripped bare to fill the house with flowers, there are no gaps to be seen in the herbaceous borders and garden that are on show. I once thought cutting gardens should have the same sort of charm as well-tended kitchen gardens: an illusion of orderliness and management in a chaotic and difficult world. But more recently I have given up on this illusion, and crave the wild. Now I want planting so closely packed with beauty that no staking is needed and weeds don't stand a chance; umbellifers striking up from a carpet of colour to touch the sky; planting that is softer and more harmonious, gentler on the eye. I want to hit that sweet spot between the naturalistic plantscapes of the wilder places of the world, and the planned and curated planting of Dutch garden designer Piet Oudolf. Soft grasses, intermingled with bold structural plants, chosen for their colour and shape. To do this, I use my boots and endless lengths of string to measure out a grid across the field. Each zone gets a plant, and each of these has no choice but to grow side by side.

When you start, know that there will be lists, frustrations, confusions and compromise, but that you will come out with something that is, at very least, a design. Whether you stick to it, whether it works, and whether it meets your needs are in the gift of the gardening gods and the weather, but these tips will at least stack the cards in your favour.

i) Find a source of pictures. This could be Instagram, books, magazines, seed packets that you have in your seed tin, or Pinterest.

ii) Start to put together the flowers you like most. This is even easier if you can find combinations of flowers that look good together. I swear by cool and warm palettes in terms of colours.

iii) Cast an eye over whether you have a mix of foliage plants, big round flowers and flowers for texture. If you only have round, your garden will be bold but have a distinctly agitating and slightly aggressive effect. Too much hefty bling. No room to breathe. Too little, though, and it will be all texture and no substance.

An easy way of getting a balance in your planting, and thus in the flowers you have available for cutting in the summer months, is to make sure that you have flowers of each shape type: focals, fillers, spires and foliage.

In my mind, sweet peas deserve a whole category of their own. Set aside a bed for these somewhere. Anywhere.

FOCALS

The big hitters. Round, beautiful, perfectly formed flowers. These will often be the thing you start with, and will determine the rest of the planting or arranging scheme.

» **Roses**
» **Dahlias**
» **Rudbeckias**
» **Cosmos**
» **Peonies**
» **Sunflowers** (I only grow Italian white because I find the traditional, big-faced sunflowers just too stiff and unwieldy)

FILLERS

If you want interest and texture, you need fillers. These are the flowers with interesting shapes and forms that lift and frame the round shapes into something special. They can be spires to punctuate or flat-headed umbellifers to soften. Extra points if they are scented as well as textural.

Umbellifers:

» **Dill**
» **Ammi**
» **Bronze fennel flowers**
» **Orlaya**
» **Cow parsley** (in early spring)

Spires:

» **Larkspur** (my favourite is smoky eyes, but if you can get hold of Earl Grey, also known as misty lavender, all the better)
» **Foxgloves**

Other great fillers:

» **Phlox**
» **Bladder campion**
» **Nigellas**
» **White corncockle**

FOLIAGE

You always need more foliage than you think. If you are cutting for the house and filling urns, jugs or vases, expect about half of the material that you cut to be foliage. It gives everything else a canvas on which to shine, and enough space for the individual focal flowers to breathe.

This is where matrix planting has the advantage. If you have a traditional cutting garden, a big block of foliage plants can look quite boring and you will be tempted to skimp and add another couple of rows of cosmos or three hybrid teas instead – something you may regret.

If you do find yourself short of some bulk, your imagination may save you – there is nothing like a bit of scarcity to invigorate the creative juices. Hedges, trees, weeds, grasses and climbers suddenly become fair game for your snips. (If you are foraging around and about, please do make sure you have permission, while cutting in parks, shared spares or council land is a definite no.) I once put proper field thistles and some dock seed heads into an oversized urn for a very grand supper club.

My favourite foliage plants:

» **Copper beech**
» **Bronze fennel**
» **Atriplex**
» **Oak**
» **Old man's beard** (aka wild clematis)
» **Bells of Ireland**
» **Pea vines** (either sweet peas or podding peas)
» **Mint**
» **Bupleurum**
» **Cinnamon basil**
» **Dill**
» **Raspberry greens**
» **Scented pelargoniums**

INTERESTING BITS

These are the bits that make your arrangements utterly unique. The bits you don't get from the buckets by the sliding doors in a supermarket. The bits that people remember. In the garden, these will be the plants that stop people in their tracks and compel them to pinch cuttings when you aren't looking. On the dinner table, they'll touch them and ask if they're real. They may even eat them, if it is that sort of evening.

My favourites:

» **Tomatoes** (the crazier the colour the better. I have grown Indigo
     Rose black ones and they never fail to arrest)
» **Runner beans** (flowers or pods)
» **White currants**
» **Wild strawberries**
» **Poppy seed heads**
» **Nasturtium vines**
» **Sloes and blackberries** (even unripe, they look wonderful. For bigger
     arrangements, plums or branches of crab apples)
» **Twigs** (useful in spring when other things haven't got going yet)

iv) Once you have your list of dream flowers, check the heights. All flowers look the same size in a seed catalogue – they are not. In photographs a *Scabiosa ochroleuca* and a *Cephalaria gigantea* appear almost identical, but the former is 50cm (20 inches) tall with tiny, alpine-like flowers and the latter grows to 2.5m (8¼ft). I have been surprised by both. One year I had a perfect mix of plants in perfect colours in the matrix planting but the atriplex and the fennel grew like weeds and soared rapidly up to almost 2m (6½ft). The subtle mix of grasses and dahlias and the odd rudbeckia didn't even get a look-in, and the chicory tried to keep up, reached above my head and then keeled over, crushing the *Erigeron annus*. Only the echinops was perfect size-wise. I am all for some tall, airy, wispy elements, but they should not dominate and they should not cast too much shade. I have since vowed to stick with punctuations of *Stipa gigantea* and the odd *Sanguisorba* 'Cangshan Cranberry'.

how to sow

Growing plants is in our blood but that doesn't mean things always turn out well. I have probably had as many things fail to grow as I have had thrive. It is not always easy to know which plants are difficult to grow, as different ones seem to like different people. I have a neighbour who can't grow cosmos for love nor money, for example. It grows like a weed for friends, family, work colleagues and everyone else, but for her it fails to get out of the ground every time. If you are in a fragile state of mind and are using horticulture as therapy, such germination failures can make you vulnerable to crashing disappointments. Not even plants want to be around you, your brain will tell you. The mind is a very egocentric thing. In these circumstances, I recommend madly over-sowing, and not starting with the tricky ones.

Following these instructions will increase your chances of success, but please be aware there are things outside of your control. No seed has a 100% germination rate and the seed you collect from your own plants will almost invariably germinate the best.

And keep in mind that sometimes things just don't work out. There's a fine line between giving up too soon and cutting your losses. I know my mental health is improved by throwing away trays of seeds that have not germinated. Their presence seems to mock me, calling into question my green fingers and my legitimacy as a flower grower. But some plants do need a long lead-up time and shoving a seed tray in the corner of the greenhouse and forgetting about it has sometimes reaped the best rewards with the trickiest of seeds. Indeed some flowers thrive on this treatment. I have grown bells of Ireland every year for ten years and the only way I get them to do anything is to freeze them for a fortnight, sow them in my best compost, inspect them daily for three weeks, be disappointed, throw them on an empty patch of soil in the flower field, curse and swear at them, and report to anyone listening that they're a waste of space and I won't bother again. 100% germination. Robust plants. Guaranteed.

Not all seeds are created equal. Some are just desperate to grow and barely need a whisper of warmth and moisture to burst vigorously and enthusiastically into life. Others need careful coaxing and persuasion and adjusted conditions to oblige. One of the simplest ways to identify easy seed is to look at your native flora. If a plant is perfectly adapted to your local climate, seasons, soil, you have won half the battle. It is already primed to succeed without you. I only have to wave some seeds of *Daucus carota* at compost and I have an abundance of solid healthy seedlings. If you are more adventurous and want to grow plants from habitats other than your own, you will have to work a bit harder to mimic their ideal conditions and create life.

As well as choosing the most suitable plants, there are other things you can do to make sure the seed is on your side, and is ready and willing to grow. Fresh seed always has better germination rates than old seed – a factor known as its viability. While this affects some types more than others (some seeds have shorter lifespans), a good general principle is to buy fresh seed every season. It is also one of the reasons why seed you harvest from your own plants seems to work so brilliantly.

How viable your seeds stay doesn't just depend on age, but also on the conditions in which they are kept. I make an effort to make the packets of the seeds I sell look attractive, and I know that lots of people pin them on the walls of their homes. This is fine for a while, but it tends to overly warm them up. Seeds like to be cool in their dormant phase. I am quite unusual in that I have a dedicated seed fridge, but I plead with you, however beautiful the packaging, keep the inner envelope of seeds in a cool dark place. This does not have to be in a fridge, but it should definitely be out of direct sunlight – definitely not on the windowsill, and definitely not in the kitchen.

My last point is one that doesn't so much affect the quality and quantity of my plants, but does make a huge difference to me. Get prepared ahead of time. I start thinking about compost in February. I am not the most organized of people, but I am also really short on time. I know that if the conditions are right on a Saturday morning when I have an hour to spend seed sowing, this is absolutely not the moment I should be getting in the car and going to a garden centre.

I also set myself up for success by giving gifts to my future self. If I have an hour when I have already put my boots on and got into the greenhouse, I don't just fill the pots I need that day, I fill and pack an extra 20, so that I can just pop out in the week and keep sowing. If I have brought a bag of compost indoors to start some seedlings on the kitchen windowsill, I'll do an extra tray.

If you don't have water outdoors, putting some filled-up pots or watering cans next to your seedlings may mean the difference between life or death on a frantic Wednesday morning when you have a million things to do and running around filling up watering cans isn't an option. Otherwise, start them in your bathroom or kitchen where you can make sure they stay moist.

There is also a school of thought that suggests that tap water that has been allowed to settle and come up to room temperature is better for watering. I make no comment on this; I just know that an appropriately watered plant (see page 54) is better than either a baked/bone-dry or drowned one.

GETTING STARTED

Just imagine. You have been given some seeds as a gift. You have such a lovely garden, they say. These will look beautiful in that border by your house, they say. We will pop round in July and see how they are getting on, they say.

You hold these tiny specks of potential life in your hand. How on earth do you convert them into a bucket of flowers. How do you turn potential happiness into actual joy?

DIRECT SOWING

This involves putting the seed straight into the soil, in the ground, where you expect it to flower. The soil needs to be clear and weeded and the time of year also matters, but it is the simplest way of sowing a seed.

At the time indicated on the packet (usually when the soil is warm), clear some ground. It should be weed free and not too lumpy. If you are at the early stages of preparing ground for sowing, please research Charles Dowding and do everything he tells you to do (I give you my no-dig process on page 75). If you are planting seeds for cutting flowers, sowing in rows is generally best. This helps you space the plants more easily and also see where the weeds are, so you can keep on top of them without accidentally damaging or disturbing the plants you want.

Water before you do anything else. Watering after sowing will disturb your carefully sprinkled seed and push your line all over the shop. Then, using a trowel, a stick or your finger, make a line in the soil. Have a label and a pen to hand before you put a single seed in the ground. You will think you will remember what you have put where, the variety and the date. You will not. Not only is it important to remember what you planted where, it helps you keep track if you have limited space. I once sowed some *Ammi majus* over a patch of disappointing Icelandic poppies. I think the soil disturbance bumped the poppies into life. The mix looked glorious by late July, but it wasn't what I intended.

A side note on labels: I find they move around a lot. I think this is because the voles disturb the soil underneath, causing them to fall over and blow around. But pheasants also peck at them and dogs occasionally steal them to play with. That is why I also try to have a notebook with me when I am planting out and add the different areas to the field plan. Even if you have only a few flower beds, it also gifts you the chance to give your areas overly romantic and bucolic names. In my field, I have 'Field-Side-North', 'Orchard-Top-South', 'Back Meadow', 'Raspberry Square', and 'Left Box'. More pragmatically, I also photograph the pages of the notebook with my phone because I know I will never be able to find the notebook when someone asks me what variety of iris I have just photographed.

The line you draw in the soil should be quite shallow, a scratch really, maybe a centimetre (½ inch) deep. (Bigger seeds need deeper lines.) Never ever just tip the seeds from the packet into the soil. You will end up with all of the seeds in a clump, however much you try and sprinkle. Tip as many of the seeds as you need out of the envelope into the cupped palm of your hand. I rarely sow all of the seeds at once. Little and often (also known as successional sowing) is a good way of hedging your bets if one set of sowing fails, gets eaten by slugs, or forms a glut all at once. This is especially so if you are not sure whether to sow inside or outside, or directly or indirectly. Try a pinch here and a pinch there.

Once you have tipped them out, use your other hand to pick the seeds up between your thumb and forefinger as if you were pinching salt or pepper, then very gently sprinkle them quite finely along the line. Do not worry at this stage about spacing, but it is likely that the eventual plants will need to be about 15cm (6 inches) apart. If you direct sow one seed every 15cm (6 inches), you are likely to get nothing because there is rarely such a high success rate. Aim to sow more thickly and then thin out or transplant once you know how many plants you have. When you have sown as many seeds as you are going to, gently move the soil from the ridges on either side of your

» Draw a line in the soil   » Sprinkle seed finely

line back into place. Press down quite gently with the palm of your hand (fingers if you are planting into modular trays with the individual cells for each seed). You need to make sure that the seed is in good solid contact with the soil and there are no big air pockets. If you do want to water at this stage, use a watering can with a rose and be quite gentle. I cannot recommend walking on your soil to press the seeds in. If you have practised no-dig (see page 75) for many years and your soil structure is exquisite, you may, but you are basically showing off.

Another side note: when you plant out seedlings or young plants watering afterwards is essential because it washes the soil particles into any potential gaps and makes sure there are no air pockets.

"The seed sowing season is the anchor of my year. I wait,
restlessly, for the air and the earth to warm and life to start.
I sow seeds with nurturance and care, faith and hope,
expectation. Seed by seed, I bring forth life."

» Use peat free seed compost to fill the tray   » Sprinkle the seed sparingly and gently

INDIRECT SOWING

Otherwise known as starting under glass. This tends to mean in a greenhouse, but in fact it means starting the germination and the first stage of the growing process in any environment where you can control the conditions. This could be a greenhouse, but there are many other options if you don't have one. I managed for a long time on kitchen windowsills and a cold frame by the backdoor.

The point of starting indoors is that by controlling (and hopefully optimizing) the heat, light, growing medium, moisture, and nutrients around the tiny seed, you can maximize its chances of growing into a mature, resilient, robust and thriving little plant ready to take on the outside world and make its own way in life.

» Label

» Water carefully using a rose

A note on light. If you are starting seeds indoors, it is a good idea to have as much light as possible. The bit of floor just inside a French window if you have one. A windowsill where you know that window catches the sun. Bathrooms can be good because they tend to be light and a bit shiny so light bounces around a lot. The downside of bathrooms is of course that their windows tend to be frosted or covered in a blind, giving quite diffuse light. I think most houses have some area that catches enough light to at least start the seeds off, but not all. Poor light will give leggy plants so if you really can't give them what they need, put them outside as often as you can or invest in grow lights. Grow lights are long, thin lamps that can be hung over the seed tray (always closer to them than you think), which makes sure that the germinating seedlings have lots of light, and so grow stocky and strong. They used to be the preserve of professional growers but there are many on the market for home gardeners now. A quick online search will reveal many options for whatever space you have.

DIRECT OR INDIRECT?

Advantages of direct sowing: I cannot deny that direct sowing is the quick and dirty way of getting plants going. If you only have ten minutes and you want to play the numbers game (that is, you have a lot of seeds and it doesn't matter if some of them do not germinate), this is the way to go. I also cannot deny that direct sowing is the most sustainable and ecologically sensitive route to abundance. Starting under glass normally involves bought compost, which almost always requires a significant amount of resources to make, transport and package.

Disadvantages of direct sowing: The germination rate is lower because the conditions are a bit harsher. You start your season later because you have to wait for the soil to warm up and even if the daytime temperatures are good, the air can still be quite chilly at night until April or so. I also find that direct-sown seeds are more vulnerable to damage from slugs, snails, rabbits, deer and pheasants. The growth is very tender in the early stages and it really doesn't take much to finish a plant off.

Advantages of indirect sowing: One of the biggest advantages for me is getting to watch the magic happen close up. That first glimpse of sharp acid green in a pot of crumbly brown compost is what makes my life worth living. Having it happen in front of my eyes is pure magic. I have been known to check seed trays on an hourly basis, just waiting for it to happen. Squash seeds are great for this, you can practically see them sprouting.

Other more practical advantages are that indirect sowing allows you to start fewer seeds and get more plants; to grow just the amount of seeds you need if you have limited space outside; and to put out plants that are likely to be much more resilient and go on to flower well. Some also say that direct-sown seeds produce stronger plants because they are better adapted to the conditions in which they will finally live. (And I can't pretend that moving from my warm kitchen and crumbly fine seed compost into the great outdoors won't be a bit of a shock.) But like so many other things, it's swings and roundabouts. Seeds started under glass will get you earlier flowers and if this matters to you, it is likely to really matter. But if it isn't a bother, waiting a bit longer and starting outdoors when the season is a bit more advanced is just as likely to give good results.

Disadvantages of indirect sowing: You are going to have to buy stuff. Starting under glass is much more resource intensive and unless you are very ingenious indeed, it is likely to involve plastic. It is also a lot more of a faff as you have to replace mother nature and provide the seeds with what they need in terms of warmth, light and moisture. I am not saying it is a particularly onerous task, but you cannot fill a greenhouse or kitchen windowsill with pots and trays of seeds ready to go and then slope off for a week to St Anton. Also, some plants dislike root disturbance so much that pricking them out and potting on isn't possible, so direct sowing is your only option. Poppies for one.

PRICKING OUT

Pricking out simply means putting each germinated seedling into its own pot. The jump from a seed tray to the great outdoors is too much for most, and a little spell of growing on in an individual pot makes all the difference. Do this when you can see the first real set of leaves appear (the first ones are false leaves, the second ones are 'true' leaves). I always use a pencil to lift the roots out of the compost gently, and I always have a row of square pots lined up ready and full of compost (this needs to be a multi-purpose or John Innes 1 rather than seed compost) to prick out into. The pencil doubles up as a dibber to make the hole to drop the seedling's roots into (gently firm it in, do not press down) and then, of course, is useful for labelling.

CONTAINERS

It is all the rage to use egg boxes and cut up plastic milk bottles. I am all
for this, but make sure there is enough depth. Roots go downwards and if
they do not have a bit of space to spread about, you will have very unhappy
plants. They also need drainage holes, so make sure you puncture these into
any plastic container you are making use of.

My policy on plastic is: use it where it can be used, and reused, and it is
effective and efficient to do so. I have a finite number of good-quality square
plastic pots that I use over and over again. They fit perfectly together in a
gravel tray to maximize the use of space. I use seed trays for small seed that
take a bit of time to get going and pots for the fast seeds that would outgrow
a tray in days or the big seeds that I sow singly. This means cosmos mostly,
and squash.

Sweet peas have their own rules. Use cardboard inner tubes, always. Mice
eat mine if I direct sow. And the best plants come from an autumn sowing.

POTTING ON

When the roots have filled the container and they start to show in the
drainage holes, it is time to give them a bit more space. And not only space,
seedlings that are growing on strongly will need more food. Your seedlings
getting yellow leaves are a sign that they have used up what they have and
it is time to step up. If the weather is kind and you have timed it right,
you might be able to plant straight out into the ground or into their final
planting place. If the plant needs a bit more protection, use a pot of the
next size up and put a layer of good peat-free multi-purpose compost in the
bottom. Carefully tip out the plant into your hand, being careful of the stem
and the root ball, and place it in the centre of the bigger pot. Carefully fill
in around the plant with the compost. Water.

⌃ Sweet peas have a long tap root and need a deep container.

≈ Cardboard will rot down in the soil and will help prevent root disturbance in planting out

SEED COMPOST

If you are the sort of person who is self-sufficient for compost and has riddling and amending seed compost down to a fine art, I will assume this guide is not for you. For the rest of us, here are some lessons I have learnt.

Two years ago, someone came to help me in the field for a few hours a week. He had been the gardener at a famous garden and I was somewhat star-struck that he was going to be here and I was keen to impress. He was due to start in April, so in March, I scrubbed out the greenhouse, laid out all the seed trays, got sowing with enthusiasm, and not a little performance anxiety. Absolutely nothing happened. A whole month, and I had some sorry-looking digitalis, and that was it. In a fit of despair, I slung the lot behind the compost heap when no one was looking, and started again.

I travel a lot with work, and my mother-in-law gives me gardening gift vouchers for Christmas and birthdays. This meant I would often stop at random garden centres and stock up on bags of seed compost. Full marks for thinking ahead, but zero for growing success. The seed compost I have bought from garden centres is generally dreadful; it is dry and sandy and bakes hard at the slightest excuse. Almost all of my failures at the germination stage (I have now stopped sowing too early) have been down to compost quality. For seed sowing, compost needs to be low in nutrients (because the seed itself holds what it needs to get going); quick draining, so the seed doesn't rot; and very crumbly and fine, so the tiny roots do not encounter any big lumps. Seek out smaller nurseries that stock good-quality compost, such as Melcourt's, or go online and get Dalefoot's or Fertile Fibre, or other organic peat-free compost. Fertile Fibre is available as biodynamic compost.

It goes without saying that any compost you buy must also be peat free. I am aware that certain leading gardening voices claim that non-peat-based mediums are less successful at growing and so we should carry on using peat-based compost in case people are put off gardening. This leaves me speechless. I would rather have a 25% germination rate, than 80% and be responsible for the destruction of a natural, irreplaceable carbon sink.

Put the bag in the greenhouse or somewhere fairly warm when you get it home, so that it is at room temperature when you come to sow.

When you tip the compost into anything it will sink more than you thought imaginable. You need to press it carefully and gently into the container, modules or seed tray to make sure it isn't all just air pockets. This is quite fiddly, but it will collapse as soon as you water it anyway, and you need to be careful you aren't burying your seeds too deeply if you have to top up again afterwards. Keep very gently pressing, especially in the corners, until you are sure the compost is even. (You can use a tamper, or wooden flat thing, to press down in seed trays, but this doesn't work for pots or modules, so just be patient.)

That said, too firm, and the tiny roots will not be able to make their way through the soil without effort, so do not tamp until the soil is hard. I have been told that the perfect texture is similar to that of a Victoria sponge. It all depends upon your baking skills I suppose…

DEPTH AND DENSITY

The general principle is that a seed should be planted at a depth of between two and three times its height. I think sowing too deep is responsible for many germination failures. Many seeds need a bit of light to spark them into life, and some don't have quite enough energy in them to reach the surface and then get going. On the other hand, if they lie on the surface of the compost, they're not quite able to anchor into the soil, so distribute fairly finely and sparsely over the surface of the soil, and then sprinkle a little compost over the top. A sprinkle, as opposed to a layer.

I often get asked about vermiculite – silvery mineral flakes that are often mixed into compost or layered on top of seed trays as a top dressing. I don't use it and don't fully understand why anyone does. Direct comparisons seem to suggest that seeds germinate better without it for me, or at the very least just as well.

WATERING

Picture the scene. A greenhouse full of tiny seedlings. I have to go away for three days for work. Not so long that I need to ask someone to come and take care of them. They'll be fine, I think. They are not. The tray under the leaking roof window is fine. Everything else is fried. Aha, I think. I will fill the trays with a little bit of water so the next time I am away for three days, they will have something to drink. Perfect. A centimetre (½ inch) or so deep around all of the seed trays. They drowned.

My advice? If you are serious about growing from seed, you cannot go away at the start of spring, or you need to find someone sensible you trust who can look in on them every single day. Water is the key thing here, but you also need to be aware if any slugs or snails are getting into your growing space, or if a sudden hot spell means your seedlings need extra shade (if indoors) or ventilation (if in a greenhouse).

I am the proud owner of about 15 grow-bag trays. These are big plastic gravel trays, about 5cm (2 inches) deep that do not have any holes. These are very cheap in my local garden centre, and you will need at least one. You will be using them for watering from beneath. This is non-negotiable. I water from beneath when I first sow seeds (often before) but also as they are growing. Any watering from the top, even with a rose, means risking damaging seedlings, or ending up with a massive dent in the middle of the compost. Sprays do not get enough moisture to where it is needed; they sort of dampen the leaves and the very top of the soil. You need to get down to where the roots are, and where the roots need to reach. To water well, fill the grow-bag tray to at least 2.5cm (1 inch) and then place the seed tray or pot in it. Leave for a few minutes – often the top of the compost will darken – lift out, drain for a few seconds, and then continue with the next one. If you have a lot of pots to do, a tray that you can fit all of your pots on to will allow you to lift them in and out in groups. But this is not a laborious job, and I find it quite satisfying.

How often should you water? Twice a week in cool weather, every other day in warm weather, every day in hot spells. More often as the plants get bigger as they will be drinking more.

APRIL

SUNDAY 26

There is new life. The Madame Alfred Carrière
rose hanging precariously on to the estate
fencing is smothered in buds and the first have
burst in the shaggy way they do. Some of the
singles have also started. The right-hand side
of the field is a cutting hedge, and now the
quinces are over, the lilacs have started. Deep
purples and delicate clotted-cream whites,
their scent catches me every time I open the
greenhouse. The *Viburnum opulus* (snowball
bush) moves a few shades up the paint chart
from lime green to clean white every day.

MONDAY 27

A flurry of activity in the village. The air has
been so still recently that you can hear the trees
move and the rustle of the cow parsley coming
through the grass. But there is rain coming,
and the lawnmowers are eager to beat it. I
finish putting in the new plants for the matrix
planting, adding phloxes and grasses to thicken
the understory. The bronze fennel is waist high
already and the opium poppies are catching up.

TUESDAY 28

We wake to the sound of thick, heavy dripping.
Thatched roofs have no gutters so the rain
comes in sheets off the ends of the straw,
sometimes channelled into gullies along the
folds of the building. I struggle when the sun is
out, because I feel I should be doing something
all the time. The rain drives me indoors to rest.
I dream of banana custard, and my friends
share their comfort-food fantasies with me.
Pear and chocolate crumble. Squash risotto.
Marmite pasta. Apple and plum crumble. Jam
sponge. Macaroni cheese. I eat none of these
things, but I recognize a need that we all have
right now for soothing, for being soothed.
Sometimes self-care looks like watching the
garden from through the kitchen window.
Sometimes it looks like calling a halt, and
just stopping.

THURSDAY 30

The Ravenswing is bent double with the weight
of water. Every plant has put on centimetres of
growth in a day. The hedges are bright, lime,
fresh green. The world feels different. Fresher.
Cleaner. I adored the early spring heatwave and
the days of endless sun, but they took their toll
on the plants. They look positively relieved. The
irises unfurl in the morning sun and their flags
sparkle with droplets of the last rain shower.
The first to come is Langport Wren, a locally
bred iris from Kelways plant nursery, as dark
and mysterious as any. Short stemmed, though.

MAY

MONDAY 4

The day is spent in the allotment, a new area of the field. An area for rows of flowers for cutting. Only the kitchen garden has rows at the moment. All my other flowers are grown in tapestries of inter-sown plants, or meadows, or in pots and planters. The allotment is bounded by a chestnut-paling fence and sits at the bottom end of the orchard. It is in the place where the compost deliveries were made, which means that it has been inadvertently no-dig for about ten years. The ground is covered with a layer of perfect, soft, clean compost. The dahlias were grown there last year, and I leave them in. Rows of species foxgloves are also starting to flower. A ready-made garden.

FRIDAY 8

Everything seems full today. The growth is fast but strong and there are new flowers out everywhere I look. I start the day strong, clearing some nettles at the far end of the apple trees, layering the new bay of the compost heap, active, strong, physical. And then the sun climbs higher and it is properly hot. The girls lie in patches of dappled shade and dip their noses in buckets of rainwater. Hugo is more dedicated and follows me around, but with the air of a spaniel who wishes I would just sit still. By midday, I do, and we climb into the hammock for an indecently long rest. Hugo adores the hammock and races to jump in it if anyone goes near it.

SATURDAY 9

A neither here nor there day. Too drizzly for serious gardening. Too dry to indulge in rainy-day activities. A compromise of tidying the greenhouse, sweeping the courtyard. I now have a Belfast sink under the tap in the greenhouse, which is disproportionately pleasing. It is filled with buckets and buckets of tulips. Some jobs are urgent, such as tying in the sweet peas and the runner beans, and erecting a mesh cover for the Tuscan kale. (I am cursed with whitefly else.) A neighbour has given me a rare form of perennial kale, Taunton Deane kale, preserved in the gardens at Knightshayes Court in Devon. It is meant to grow into something that resembles a tree and she describes it as 'more cattle feed than cavolo nero' but I have been trying to source one for some time, and I am delighted to see it. Until then, pea tops, wild garlic, and home-made pasta form the mainstay of meals.

SUNDAY 10

There are the fun bits of gardening, and then there is the weeding. For the first time I think in my life, I have spent so much time weeding that I feel almost on top of it. There is one bit I have been neglecting, and that is under the apple espaliers. The odd tulip pops up there which is my excuse to leave it alone in April, which means by May, it is a jungle. A *Cerinthe* has self-seeded there and it is the only plant reliably smothered in bees, further postponing any intervention.

when to sow

Too early: We've all been there. Or at least I have. The winter is long, it is dull. Instagram starts to fill with pictures of blossom and narcissi and I have a little panic. Everyone else seems to be so on top of things, so organized, so active. I rush out and start sprinkling seeds on anything that can hold soil. I haven't planned or prepared properly, it is willy-nilly and scatter-gun. Worse, the season is not ready. There needs to be enough light for seedlings to thrive. I can provide the heat (see page 60) but I cannot provide the light and I have no intention of getting grow lights. Seeds germinate indoors very early in the season, but then they are checked (stopped from moving smoothly through their stages of development and growth) if they are left in pots or trays too long, or are pricked out when their roots systems are too advanced. Oh, and seed just chucked on the ground when the soil is damp and cold will sit and rot. If you don't want to have your hands in it, seeds don't want to be in it either.

Too late: I am busy. Like, unbelievably busy. I try not to go on about it because it is so tedious and, actually, I don't know anyone who isn't busy. There have been some weeks when I think: Ah yes, now would be the perfect time for putting those sweet peas in, or I really must not direct-sow the ammi because of the rabbits, so I'll do it in pots. I start every weekend with great intentions and then somehow… The good news is that this only matters if you are growing for a special date, or if you are trying to get flowers evenly spread across the season. In fact, nature is very, very forgiving and the guidance for hardy annuals is early to mid spring, so if you are sowing in late-ish spring, you really aren't too far behind the curve.

My flower field in south-west England is very mild and really quite damp. I have roses flowering at Christmas, and my rudbeckias and dahlias frequently over-winter in the ground. This means that I can sow seeds at all sorts of funny times and get late flowers, and it really doesn't matter. However, there are reasons why you shouldn't leave it until the height of summer. The ground is much drier later on, and the rate of growth is a little slower. Make sure you have primed your soil for really good growing, and make sure you water consistently.

Hardy annuals (plants that are not killed by frost) have two options. They can germinate, grow, flower, set seed and die all in one season, or they can germinate, and grow in the autumn of one season, and then flower earlier the next year. If you want to get everything in one year, sow in spring. If you would like them to over-winter, sow in late summer/early autumn. Sowing in between means they get a bit 'stuck' between the options, and will panic as the cold weather comes in. You will end up with some not very happy-looking flowers in early winter.

Where I live, the spring equinox marks the time of most seed-based activity. Growth is rapid and strong. Generally, the last frost is passed. However, the official Somerset last frost date is in April, and two years ago we had snow at the end of March. So if you can't rely on the calendar date, how do you know when to sow? Answer: you need to use your senses. When the time's right the air will smell different, the weeds will germinate rapidly, absolutely everything will be growing. I generally do sweet peas first (if they haven't been overwintered), then hardy annuals indoors, then hardy annuals outdoors, then half-hardy annuals indoors, and then finally half-hardy annuals outdoors.

greenhouses

It is half-past three. I visit the greenhouse for the fourth time today. There is an enveloping warmth of trapped sunshine. A warmth that bathes the bones. The smell of growth, and compost, and seeds, and damp gravel. On my right, the heat mat is covered with a jigsaw of pots, trays, tubs and modules, each fitted carefully together to make the most of its magic warmth. Cinnamon basil, woad for dyeing, Tête Noir red cabbages, trays of thyme, chard, beetroot and some hopeful wild strawberries (the seed was ancient, I am managing my expectations).

The heat mat changed everything for me. It is a long strip of foil with heating elements snaking up and down. Crucially, it is thermostat controlled, and a pleasingly copper probe ensures that I can keep my seed trays at a constant 18-20°C (64-68°F). This is particularly important at this early stage of the season as the chilly nights (it is forecast to be close to freezing tonight) can check growth, even when the daytime conditions are perfect for getting everything sprouting.

It's not the only way, though. I used windowsill propagators for years with great success. But make sure you use the clear plastic lids with these. I do find them very drying.

And if you don't fancy one of those either, I have grown hundreds of kilos of pumpkins and squash from plants started on a storage heater. I was freezing during the winter, but they were worth keeping just for that.

It is a quarter to five. I visit the greenhouse for the fifth time today. More cosmos has sprouted – it really is the fastest seed to germinate. A single copper stock seed (*Matthiola incana*) shows a little green. I sprinkle a little more compost on the beetroot. I dip the seed tray of thyme in a tray of water just in case it is a bit dry. Weighing the tray in your hands gives a better indicator than poking and prodding. Compost that is dry feels too light.

I tip compost into a tray, shake to level, press very gently. I have been known to over-compact my compost and you can tell, because the roots tend to sit on the surface and go sideways rather than heading down. They look sort of insecure in the compost. Seeds that are not sufficiently covered with compost will also struggle, and often dry out too quickly. TV gardener Monty Don just does a sort of tap to settle the compost. But I do prefer a little more pressure.

Once sprouted, the trays move to the other side of the staging. Some pricked out, some just waiting and growing. Rows and rows of tomatoes. Ammi. Cavolo nero. Kelvedon Wonder peas. Leeks. I thought the germination had been poor, but once off the heat, a new leek seedling has appeared every day for about three weeks. I stroke the plants gently to strengthen the stems. (Plants in a greenhouse are protected from moving air – it's the equivalent of running on a treadmill where you're free from wind resistance. Stroking them mimics this moving air and is also astonishingly therapeutic.)

The plants that are getting ready to be planted out sit on the path by the door, hardening off. A few days outside, and then I will pick a spell of even, warm weather and plant them into the kitchen garden.

The greenhouse was a secondhand one, moved from the Old Vicarage, on the other side of the church to me, many years ago. I cannot pretend it is particularly pretty, but I do adore it. Nor can I pretend it is particularly sturdy – it has been blown away more times than I care to count. The wind comes in the door if it is left open and pops the glass out. Once the glass has gone, the frame isn't very strong at all, and it just crumples in the most dramatic and tragic way. I now check it religiously if I hear the slightest breeze, often padding out in my pyjamas so I can sleep soundly when the wind is howling.

jobs for spring

SOW ANNUAL SEEDS

PRICK OUT

PICK TULIPS

CLEAR AND WEED BEDS
FOR DIRECT SOWING

WASH WINDOWS ON GREENHOUSE

WEED

III.
EARLY SUMMER:
GROWTH & PROMISE

JUNE

WEDNESDAY 17

Middling sort of day. Too hot with a jumper. Too cold without. Thinned the self-sown nigella in the top beds. Harvested remaining honeywort seed. Left the rest to fall and grow on for another crop in the autumn. Sowed one last line of *Ammi majus*. It is said that seed sown before the summer solstice will flower this year, seed sown after will overwinter and flower in the spring.

THURSDAY 18

A trip to Bath on a grey day. Stopped in Queen Square to photograph the trees against the stone. Coffee at Colonna & Small's. Drove home in the rain wondering if it will be dry enough to mow the orchard ever again. *Papaver nudicaule* becoming prolific, especially oranges. Potted on verbascum, more briza, Rupert's Pinks.

FRIDAY 19

Pulled first beetroot from the kitchen garden. Blue nigella out in drifts in the field. Tips of the sweet peas showing colour and are inspected almost hourly. Planted *Moluccella laevis* seedlings straight out into beds. Second sowing had much higher germination rates.

SATURDAY 20

More rain in the morning, but muggy. Talk of thunder. There are sheep in the back field and avoiding them on the dog walk led us past a bank of honeysuckle. Smelled it before I saw it. Evening – launch party at The Lyme Bay café, while Mr Alexander swam in the sea. Much champagne. Lovely chat.

SUNDAY 21

First sweet pea fully out. Valerie Harrod? Absolutely beautiful. Also first Black Ball cornflower. Pinched out the cosmos Purity in cutting beds. Mulched new beech hedge.

MONDAY 22

No work today. A wedding on Brighton bandstand. Scorching blue skies. Bride wore gold sequins. More champagne. Home very late to ecstatic dogs.

TUESDAY 23

Expected sunshine but got rain again. Dug out top beds. Cleared sweet rocket, which had reached 1.8m (6ft) and fallen on everything else. Cut pods for drying. Packed meadow seed for a September wedding in Italy. Deadheaded roses.

a meditation
on weeding

Like nephologists have many words for clouds, I often think that gardeners
should have a language that reflects the nuances and distinctions encountered
in the task that we call weeding.

There is the elatedly satisfying hoe – when the soil is dry, the weeds are
tiny, and you just have to tickle them to disrupt the roots. They say the best
hoeing is done before you can see the weeds, but if you have the inclination
to weed clean soil, you don't have enough to do. But clearing that soft green
flush, knowing you have saved yourself a much bigger job later on, and made
space for your plants to thrive and grow into the space (check under their
leaves for stray seedlings), makes you feel you're on top of things. Light,
happy, easy weeding. Choose a hot day so the weedlings dry out. If it rains
too soon and the conditions are clement, they will root again and recover.

The next part requires you, if you can, to kneel. If I am in for the long haul
and the task is large, I have been known to upturn a bucket and sit on it
to save my knees. I take a trug, sometimes two, and a daisy grubber. Every
gardener will have a favourite tool they maintain is the only way. I know
some who swear by a good hand fork, some a trowel. I even know one who
uses a bread knife. What you need is something you can get roots out with,
while disturbing the soil the least and removing as much of the plant as you
can. Weeds are tricky though, and will resist. Some have deep roots (docks);
some have travelling, invasive networks of roots that break as soon as you
touch them, making them impossible to get out completely (ground elder,
bindweed, couch grass). Some fight back with stings and prickles (nettles and
thistles). You may need gloves. But you need to keep on top of it, because if
you let it go too far, you will have a wasteland on your hands.

And why two trugs? Because, as I have mentioned, I am obsessive about my compost heap (see page 138) and make sure it heats up, which is meant to kill most weed seeds and perennial roots. However, I do not trust bindweed not to come back invigorated by the experience, so that goes into a bucket for putting out with the green waste recycling. Everything else goes onto the heap.

If your soil has gone to the wasteland stage, you either have to get digging, or spend some time not digging. The latter option is infinitely better for the soil, giving cleaner, easily healthier ground in the long term, but I cannot pretend it is a quick fix.

No-dig means just that. Instead of turning any of your soil over, you put compost and organic matter on the surface (known as 'mulching') and let the worms and the soil's natural microorganisms do the rest. This feeds the soil and, if the mulch is thick enough, will kill off all the weeds for you. It is really that simple.

The principle behind no-dig is that digging and disturbing soil damages its natural, adaptive, delicate structure. This not only means that it can compact and become less amenable to growth, but also that it breaks up and exposes mycorrhizal fungi to the air, meaning that your plants and flowers cannot get as many nutrients from the soil.

All of my growing areas, from the big field to the kitchen garden (which was, until a few short years ago, the back lawn), were brought into cultivation using no-dig. In the field, we dug out the scrub trees, the field maples and

the hawthorns, and had a bonfire. I marked out edges between paths and
beds with tent pegs and baler twine, hoarded cardboard, and asked my local
farmer for a trailer-load of well-rotted manure. This really is the biggest
downside to no-dig in my mind – you do need a huge amount of organic
matter to get going. And if you are just getting going yourself, it is unlikely
that you have a productive compost heap yet. You need to start by laying a
deep layer of compost over the beds, on top of a layer of cardboard. This first
round of compost needs to be deep enough to smother the weeds and the
grass, or whatever you have in the ground already – 15cm (6 inches) or so.
If you can get your hands on this much mulch, your growing season will be
off to a flying start. Your local recycling centre is likely to be able to deliver
green waste if required, but it will have been heat treated. This is excellent
for killing off any weeds and pathogens in it, but I do find it leaves it a little
desiccated and inert. Getting a bit of life into it (see page 94) is key.

And the amount you need for no-dig in flat beds is nothing compared to
what you need for raised beds. I am not a fan of raised beds; I have tried
them, but I cannot get beyond the fact that wooden edges are an absolute
haven for slugs.

my one-year no-dig plan

EARLY SPRING

» Mow grass as short as possible.

» Take measurements of ground and map-out beds and paths.
  Paths are 50cm (20 inches) wide and beds 2m (6½ft) wide.

» Transfer plan to ground using sticks and baler twine.

» Put layer of thick cardboard on beds, edges overlapping on to the paths.

» Spread a layer of well-rotted farmyard manure over the beds, keeping
  the layer around 8cm (3 inches) thick.

» Spread layer of green waste compost over the manure about
  8cm (3 inches) thick.

» Spread thinner layers over the paths, supplemented with some
  wood chippings from a local tree surgeon.

MID SPRING

» Sow seeds and plug plants straight into top layer of compost.

SUMMER

» Keep plants watered.

» Remove weeds with light hoeing.

» Ease out docks that come up through the cardboard and mulch
  layers by the root with as little soil disturbance as possible.

» Harvest spring-sown annuals, and sow second
  crop immediately. Cut back perennials.

AUTUMN

» Carry out second harvest of flowers.

» Top-dress beds with a thin layer of home-made garden compost,
  or sow with phacelia, a fast-germinating and fast-growing plant,
  as a green manure.

I did not have enough manure and green waste in the spring to do all of the areas that I wanted to start growing in, so I pegged landscape fabric down and left it there for a year. This proved excellent at getting rid of the persistent field weeds, but did tend to attract slugs. The soil also felt a bit compressed when I removed it in the spring of the second year. But with a thin layer of top dressing, it came instantly back to life. In short, it took much longer, but needed less organic matter to get the soil to the point where I could grow on it as I wanted.

The field was brought into growing many years ago, and the odd autumnal top dressing has kept the soil in great heart. In the kitchen garden, a much more recent addition, I was a bit short of top dressing and spread it a bit thinner in some areas than I should have. I can tell the difference just by looking. The texture of these areas is rougher, they always need more weeding (although I'm still digging field bindweed out from the whole area), and they just don't grow as well.

LATE JUNE

WEDNESDAY 24

Everything seems full today. The growth is
fast but sturdy and there are new flowers out
everywhere I look. I start the day strong,
clearing some nettles at the far end of the apple
trees, layering the new bay of the compost
heap – active, strong, physical. And then the
sun climbs higher and it is properly hot. The
setters lie in patches of dappled shade and dip
their noses in buckets of rainwater. Hugo is
more dedicated and follows me around, but
with the air of a spaniel who wishes I would
just sit still. By midday, I do, and we climb
into the hammock for an indecently long rest.
Hugo adores the hammock and races to jump
in it if anyone goes near. Morag and Maud are
less enthusiastic, but can be persuaded. (Setters
are sleeping machines, and they are never more
comfortable than when they are on top of
someone.)

The day slows after the busy morning, and
by evening, there is nothing to do but watch
the moon rise over the hill.

THURSDAY 25

Refreshing the weather forecast rarely changes
its predictions, but I try. There is a frost
predicted for early next week. I generally
consider the last frost date to be mid April, as
the field lies in a particularly sheltered valley in
a particularly warm county. I have grown more
pumpkin seedlings than is any way appropriate
for a non-commercial operation, but they are
one of my absolute favourite things to grow
and eat. I had been planning on planting them
straight out into the pumpkin patch, 30cm
(12 inches) deep with well-rotted manure.
I cannot risk it. I just can't. Although some
gardeners will direct-sow squash now, I am
firmly convinced that it is too late. Also,
I sowed all my pumpkins just before the start
of spring and they are starting to suffer in their
little square pots (yellow leaves a dead giveaway
sign of stress), so there is nothing for it but
to pot on. Squash and pumpkins are hungry
plants and so I had already sown them into
multipurpose compost. Seed compost has very
little nutritional value and is only really good
at getting seeds through the germination stage.
They then need pricking out into something
more sustaining. Pumpkins germinate fast and

need that feeding, plus they don't like root disturbance much, so it makes sense to just sow them straight into multipurpose. Unfortunately they have outgrown their pots. What's more, the compost I used doesn't seem to have had any nutritional value at all, so they are starting to look a bit wan. Potting up is a satisfying and slightly repetitively mindless process. Perfect.

FRIDAY 26

There are the fun bits of gardening, and then there is the weeding. For the first time in my life, I have spent so much time weeding that I feel almost on top of it. There is one bit I have been neglecting, and that is under the apple espaliers. The odd tulip pops up there, which is my excuse to leave it alone in spring, which means by the time summer approaches, it is a jungle. A cerinthe has self-seeded there and it is the only plant reliably smothered in bees, further postponing any intervention. But intervene I must and I decide to cut down the nettles and couch grass and cover with Mypex (black landscape fabric) for a year. This no-dig method gets rid of most of the weeds while preserving the soil's structure and integrity. Next spring I can top-dress with a few centimetres of compost and use it as a space for growing, rather than letting the weeds choke the trees.

Most weeds do not take a full year to disappear and can be suppressed just using cardboard and compost, which is what I have done in most of the field. But I know there is ground elder here and you need to be a bit assertive with that sort of thing.

This is one of the jobs that is a gift to my future self, and I know I will be grateful next year. More immediately, many of the seeds that I have sown in the last fortnight are starting to come up. I took a punt on some very old leek seed and the grass-like shoots are now showing among the poppies that have appeared every time I get a hoe out. Every beech plant is now covered in the most perfect leaves. A tray of *Pennisetum macrourum* (African feather grass) seed has sprung up overnight.

There is mowing to be done, and a bonfire of clippings and woody stems too thick for the compost to be lit. Then there is pizza in the wood oven, home-made goat's cheese, and the deep satisfaction of a field set fair.

SATURDAY 27

The morning feels warm, and there is no sign of frost on the ground. The air is golden in the early sunlight and I regret being so trusting in the pronouncements of meteorologists. It is only later in the day that I see that the dahlia leaves have been blackened and the runner beans crumpled. The dahlias have overwintered in the new beds now surrounded with chestnut paling, and I am sure they will recover quickly and grow on. More of an issue at this stage of their growth is slugs. There is a time when the slugs' eating and the dahlias' rate of growth is so finely balanced that nothing seems to be happening. As the soil starts to warm up, the dahlias put on a spurt and then nothing can stop them. Except deer, obviously.

SUNDAY 28

A cup of coffee in the paddock is now a habit after lunch. On brave days, I drink it in the hammock, but am so often joined by the spaniel that it is rarely safe to do this. There is a far-off hum that sounds like a chainsaw, or maybe a mower, and it takes me some minutes to notice that the greenhouse and asparagus bed are under a dark, circling cloud of bees. They seem intent on something and not interested in us, so we just watch them for a while. When I come back an hour later (I drink a lot of coffee), they have gone and the air is clear. The noise, however, remains. I follow the sound and find that they have settled on the fence post just outside the greenhouse door, in the middle of a lilac hedge. They are on the south side of the fence in the back field, making the most of the afternoon's warmth. I am offered a neighbour's old hive, and helpful suggestions are made about cardboard boxes, and how to capture the swarm in a sheet. Discussions are had about where the hive might be placed and which of my flowers they might like and from whom I could get a suit. I do not know much about bee-keeping, but I know it is an endeavour fraught with the potential for heartbreak and difficulty and deadly bee diseases, and I cannot bear such emotional jeopardy. After some tricky post-tapping and manoeuvring by more experienced bee handlers than me (expert advice was sought), they have found a new home.

supports & structures

The best gardens have height. Punctuations of verticals that stop the garden looking flat and boring. Variations in plants can do this and climbers do it best of all. An avenue of wigwams of sweet peas in an English garden in high summer is hard to beat.

But plant supports have another use in the cut-flower world. Flowers that flop in a border are neither here nor there in the scheme of things, although a flat delphinium is a disappointing sight. However, if you are growing flowers for cutting, tall strong stems are important, and this means keeping the plants as upright as possible. Most flowers will turn towards the light and so if they are flat on the ground, the stem makes a right-angled bend towards the sky. I am all for a bit of a bend and imperfection in my flowers (known in the flower trade as 'movement'), but I've yet to find a perpendicular stem that can be made to look beautiful. The only thing to do is to cut it off at the corner and have a short stem, and promise to be earlier with the staking next season.

Staking before you need to stake is good advice. It may seem like a job you can put off, but a flopped plant can often snap off at the base and not recover. The other thing that I have discovered is that building wigwams and arches in spring when the ground is soft and the wood is pliable can be an easy and pleasant job. Leave it until the summer and, if your ground is anything like mine, it will be baked hard.

What supports you use will depend on the materials you have available and the weight and habit of the plant you are staking.

WIGWAMS, ARCHES AND TUNNELS

To make a wigwam, push six (eight if you are going for a really big wigwam) wooden rods into the soil in a circle formation, then tie them all together at the top. For an archway, sink two rods spaced apart into the soil, then fasten them at the top to form a triangle shape, or bend them onto one another to form a soft curve. You can make a tunnel by lining up several of these triangles in a row. Use wigwams in beds, and use archways and tunnels to exploit the growing space at the sides of paths. I use them primarily for sweet peas, but Cobaea, runner beans and Akebia also suit. Essentially, anything that is quite light and vine-like. You can use either hazel or willow rods, but I prefer the former as they are less regular looking. They don't last forever, about two years is my guess, depending on the weather (very hot weather makes them crack and weaken) and I recommend making sure you have a good length of stick below ground, 30cm (12 inches) or so, otherwise any structure will sway precariously for the rest of the season. If your ground is quite hard generally, a hammer and a metal rod can help you make the hole before you push the wood in. Rods just snap if you try to force them too much into hard ground.

Be aware that willow pushed straight into the ground is likely to root. If you want a living sculpture, that's fine, but it is an assertive plant, drains ground, and gets very big indeed. Willow needs to be completely dried out before it's let anywhere near soil to make sure it doesn't do this.

SOURCING HAZEL

One of the other reasons I love using hazel is that I grow a lot of it. As much
as Somerset is willow country, I find it grows like a weed for me. When
I first had the field I planted a beautiful avenue of many different coloured
willow trees along the eastern edge. An effective windbreak is necessary for
tall, elegant stems in flower growing and I wanted something fast growing
to protect the new beds. Two things happened: the really beautiful damson
and deep-red shades faded away and the yellow and lime green willows
dominated, and it turned out that the wind comes down the slope of the
Blackdowns from the south. Even with coppicing every Christmas for
wreaths, the trees grew increasingly out of control and blocked, not the
wind, but the view from the field across the valley to Pickeridge Hill.
Digging them out was far harder than putting them in (see page 176).

A cutting hedge was planted along the south side. Three colours of lilac, four
mock orange trees, an understory of Japanese quinces. And hazels, lots of lots
of hazels. Some varieties were chosen for their taste: a Pearson's Prolific and
a Lambert's filbert, but the majority are just common hazels. They are in their
seventh year now, and ready for their first big harvest. I will cut every third
tree, getting the rods from as low on the plant as I can, cutting all of the
stems that are thicker than a pencil. (This is best done between mid autumn
and the start of spring when the plant is dormant, but later harvests seem
to work as well – it just means rather laboriously stripping off the leaves.)
I only do every third tree because I still value the shelter, and I secretly
adore collecting the nuts from the trees.

CUTTING-GARDEN WHOLE BED SUPPORTS

If you need to support a whole bed and the flowers are quite light and well behaved (think larkspur and scabious, but cosmos at a push), you can't go too far wrong with string. Many people used to use plastic netting but it is quite fine and I worry about birds getting stuck. And unless you painstakingly untangle it at the end of the season, it really is a single-use item. With natural twine, you can cut down what flowers are left after the peak is over, or pull the whole plants out, and then compost everything. This is my favourite way of supporting flowers, mostly because it is like an oversized game of cat's cradle. You can buy the string ready-knotted as jute netting, but I have seen some clever people make their own. I use the netting horizontally for supporting upright stems, and vertically for sweet peas.

« Cosmos supported by horizontal netting

» Mild steel rusts beautifully   » Bend to a U-shape

steel supports

YOU WILL NEED

» **6mm (¼ inch) mild steel rods, around 3m (10ft) long**

» **A round object for shaping, such as a tree or large pot**

» **Two planks**

For big plants that are lean and quite brittle, steel semi-circles are perfect. I use these for tall perennials, but also for peonies and anything that falls over the path. Cutting gardens are soft and romantic and wild on sunny days, but you can get remarkably wet pushing your way through rain-soaked flowers. Supports are needed to keep plants upright and safe, even in inclement conditions. I also think rusting steel blends in so much better than wobbly canes and string. Credit to Monty Don who taught me this.

You will need some mild steel rods of either 6mm or 8mm (¼–⅜ inches) diameter. A length of 2.5m (8¼ft) is about right. You will likely have a local steel merchant or metal worker who can provide you with them, but there are also some good suppliers online. You will also need something round with a diameter that fits the size of the semi-circle you want to create. Big plants that are just sagging to one side will be fine with a shallow arc; plants that are going to go off in all directions (peonies) will benefit from an almost full circle. I have used many different things to get the shape I need: trees, oversized terracotta pots, a laundry bucket. You will also need two planks, or a single plank and a hard, flat surface.

» Use a plank to bend up the ends to form legs   » Push the legs deep into the ground to give strength

Find the centre point of the rod and gently bend it around your shape. It will spring back a little so over-bend a bit. You are aiming for a rough U-shape. If it feels like hard work, move your hands down towards the ends of the rods and you'll have a bit more leverage. The 6mm (¼ inch) rods bend easily; I use the 8mm (⅜ inch) ones and they do take a bit of effort, but the result is all the more satisfying for that.

To make the legs, place the curved rod flat on one of the planks with the top of the U towards you. Place the second plank flat on top. Move the second plank around a bit until you are happy that this is the point that you want the bend. Closer to the bend will mean a smaller arc to hold the plant but ultimately a taller support (good for willowy verbena or a tall sanguisorba). If you move the plank downwards towards the ends of the bent rod, you will have much more space for the foliage, but it will be shorter (good for dahlias or a flopping aster). Put your foot on the second plank to hold it steady and lift the legs up towards you. Aim for a right-angled bend. Bending the metal from quite low will keep the bend neat. Repeat as desired. Experiment until you have a set of supports that you will use and love. They will last forever, and make great presents.

a brief introduction to Korean Natural Farming

If I had one piece of advice for you, it would be to invest in your soil. Soil is a complex and wondrous miracle, a web of life. Anything you can do to support its vitality is going to improve the health of your flowers. Tradition dictates that we feed our plants by identifying the nutrients they might need and adding them in. If you want leaf growth, add nitrogen. Better roots and flowers, phosphorus. Fruit ripening needs more potassium.

But I am starting to think there is more to it than that. In the same way that you can't meet all your nutritional needs with a vitamin tablet, you can't fully nourish your soil by injecting a few specific substances. You need to think more holistically. You need to consider the soil biome.

In particular, this means the soil's network of mycorrhizal fungi, which forms an interface between the plant roots and the earth. If your soil is particularly poor, you can add fungi to help the plants access the nutrients around them. However, Korean Natural Farming (KNF) suggests not just any fungi will do. You need to add the bacteria and fungi that already thrive in your climate, your area, your conditions and your soil: the indigenous microorganisms (IMOs). Rather than mass produced and bought in a packet or a bottle, these microorganisms are specific to you, and so need to be collected from your garden, increased and multiplied through a process of fermentation, and then applied to the soil to increase its microbial health.

I am still learning about KNF and the ways plant growth and soil health can be supported by fermentation. But I have already had great success using the most basic IMO, cultured lactic acid bacteria (LAB). LAB is effective in promoting strong plant growth by aiding decomposition in soil and compost, increasing the nutrients available to plants.

The technique is best used in the early stages of the season when growth is getting going, and is even more effective when combined with fermented plant juice (FPJ). If you can make comfrey tea, you can make FPJ.

fermented plant juice foliar feed

YOU WILL NEED

» **2–3 handfuls of chopped plant material**

» **Brown sugar or molasses (equal to the weight for your chopped plant material)**

» **A large jar**

» **Cheesecloth or kitchen paper**

» **Spray bottle**

» First, collect plant material based on what stage your plants are going through. If it is spring and everything is in full growth, nettle tips or young, soft weeds. If the season is late and you want to support fruiting, windfall apples or tomatoes that have gone over. It's best to do this on a dry day, and do not wash anything you collect – the fermentation will need the wild yeasts and bacteria on the plants.

» Next, mix the chopped plant material with an equal weight of brown sugar or molasses. Cover lightly and leave for between seven and 14 days. It should begin to smell a bit vinegary-sweet, like a sourdough starter.

» Strain the liquid off and bottle. You can compost the leftover plant material. If possible, keep your FPJ in the fridge. Use it as a foliar feed – that is, spray it on the leaves – by diluting it down to one part FPJ to 1,000 parts water.

---

create your own lab culture

YOU WILL NEED

» **Two cups organic brown rice**

» **A large jar**

» **Cheesecloth or kitchen paper**

» **600ml (2½ cups) organic milk**

» Wash two cups of organic brown rice in two cups of water. Keep swirling it until the water is quite cloudy.

» Pour off the water into a jar and cover with cheesecloth or kitchen paper. Leave in a warm place out of direct sunlight for two or three days until you can smell a sweet smell. This is the rice-wash water starting to ferment. You might get a layer or mat of solids on the top, which is fine, but make sure you discard it.

⌃ Wash organic brown rice in water

» Fill another jar two-thirds full of milk, about 600ml (2½ cups). I use organic, full-fat cow's milk. Add some of the rice-wash water so there is a ratio of about one part rice water to ten parts milk. Put some cheesecloth on top and leave in the warm place again.

» The milk will start to separate into a thick layer of solids on top and a clearish fluid, the LAB, underneath. This is likely to take 48 hours or so, but it will be quicker in a warm room and slower if it's cold. It is the clear fluid you want but be careful not to disturb any of the solids into it when you lift them out. Apparently, this solid layer makes excellent cheese, but I have not been brave enough to try it.

» So far I have used the LAB by adding it to watering cans in a ratio of one part LAB to 1,000 parts water and putting it on soil next to plants, or on new compost heaps to help get them started.

≈ Add rice water to organic whole milk   ≈ After a few days, the mixture will separate

jobs for early summer

————————

DIRECT-SOW ALL FLOWERS

START SUCCESSIONAL SOWING

HARVEST ALL SUMMER FLOWERS

KEEP ON TOP OF STAKING

KEEP ON TOP OF WEEDING

PLANT OUT TENDER PLANTS AFTER LAST FROST:
DAHLIAS, RUDBECKIAS, COSMOS

TIE IN SWEET PEAS

APPLY COMPOST TEA, FERMENTED
PLANT JUICE, AND LAB

————————

IV.
LATE SUMMER:
FRIENDSHIPS, FESTIVALS, FEASTS

AUGUST

THURSDAY 27

The squash plant has grown up through next door's apple tree. The apples have codling moth damage and the squash is fruiting, so I am letting the squash do what it likes. The apple is an old Bramley, and will easily take the weight. The weather has turned. The girls come back from their walks wet up to their shoulders from the heaviness of the dew. Morag catches a rabbit. The pheasant poults are released in the wood and drive the girls to distraction.

FRIDAY 28

A day off work to prepare for the weekend's family party. Weeding, mowing, setting up the trestle tables. Finding the cake stand. The kitchen garden is replete with chard and sweetcorn. The courgettes have slowed down but everything else is ripening and fat. I stew plums from the orchard.

SATURDAY 29

The sweet pea tunnel is a golden tangle of seed pods. I let them go to seed early and wasn't expecting any more flowers, but there is a last flush of colour. The Valerie Harrod is a hot pink. This late in the season, the petals are slightly mottled, but I love them all the more for it.

My cottage is tiny, but many of the blue lias stones that make it are large. By the fire, the date 1589 is carved, and the name Edward. Maybe the cottage is that old (it is not far off) but maybe the stones were once part of the old church. The cottages are so close that the yew in the graveyard hangs over our gardens; the track into the flower field hugs three sides of the churchyard; and if the congregation look to their right, they can see the low-slung thatch of the cottages just outside the window. We got married in the church. The envelope that arrives annually for the church flowers rota is the only post I have ever received that addresses me by my husband's surname. It never occurred to them I wouldn't change my name. We did that thing of going to church in the run-up to the wedding, and haven't been back since. Supplying it with flowers for a fortnight in the height of dahlia season is the least I can do for a building so entwined with my own life. A set of keys is dropped through the letterbox and I am invited into the intimate spaces. The cupboards and the vestry. The notes left for each other that only make sense to those in the know. The elderly oasis used over and over again until it crumbles (I pointedly ignore it, obviously). I fill an urn with chicken wire and my muddy and muted collection. Branches of bronze fennel, spots of rudbeckia Sahara, softened with stems of Crème Brûlée phlox. The light inside the church is minimal, and it does not make for good photos, but I hope you get the gist.

(If you are growing Phlox in a container, and I hope you are because the stem length is incredible that way, it may need a seaweed feed. Mine is still flowering brilliantly, but it's looking a bit pale.)

garden party

We had always known we would marry in the orchard. We planted trees years ahead knowing where there would be gaps between them for the long trestle tables. We trained the apple trees into espaliers knowing that they would form the wall under a canvas roof. We would marry in August so there would be apples on the trees and hazelnuts and fat rose hips in the hedge.

And we did. Although technically we married in the church next door. We married with a best woman in bare feet (the vicar said we were all too tall) and Morag came up the aisle with us (yes, we walked into church together), her collar edged with hydrangea florets and soft raw silk ribbon. I carried hot chocolate roses and white cosmos and bronze fennel. Our nephews made their own buttonholes from Atriplex and dark scabious. We had a reading from a text by Alain de Botton and, as we ran down the track back to the orchard, our family and friends threw David Austin rose petals collected that morning by my mother. We toasted with kir royales made from cassis from the kitchen-garden blackcurrants and ate on tables lined with bottles of flowers cut at dawn.

I am an inveterate introvert and it is rare that I invite people into the intimacy of my flower field. As soon as I see it through the eyes of others, I start to see its flaws. The weeds, areas that have turned wild, the patches where things are coming on, the patches that are over. The yard that needs sweeping, and the old buckets and watering cans hastily shoved under the hedge. I grow dissatisfied and slightly panicky. A feeling only assuaged by the activity of laying the table or lighting the pizza oven. Shuttle runs between the garden and the kitchen with glasses and ice and linen napkins and trays of baby potatoes and platters of salad. The children invariably want to help, usually by walking the dogs round and round the flower beds and teaching them tricks with the crusts of bread. My family has a tradition of 'going round the garden' as soon as we arrive anywhere, and this provides the perfect opportunity to find stems and grasses to go on the table in bottles.

The last-minute job that just finishes everything off. The last thing to do before the champagne is opened and the party begins.

Maud can hear the pop of a cork from 50 paces, and her joyous rolling around in the grass with the cork always gets any festivity off to an appropriately raucous start.

_____

dressing a table

YOU WILL NEED
» **Snips**

» **Buckets of water**

» **1–3 stems of seasonal flowers and foliage for each bottle, bowl or vase**

» **Vines, fruits, vegetables or seedheads**

» **Assorted bottles, bowls and vases, one per guest**

» **Candles and candlesticks**

Summer parties in a garden need little dressing. The setting is as much the decoration as anything else. This is the peak of abundance, with colour and scent and tumbling textures everywhere you look. My dahlia beds are in full throat by late summer and if I keep up with cutting them, they will stay that way until they slow down as autumn sets in. If the roses have been fed and there have been days of cool and wet and weeks of high heat, they should be picking up for a second flush around the same time. Madame Alfred Carrières are particularly generous like this, and they soar up from the estate fencing by the back gate, welcoming us home.

» Successional sowing is key here: the early sown annuals have set seed and are over now, but the ones that were scattered later in spring are taking their place. By the end of summer, I may even get flowers from the seeds dropped by the early sown annuals, two cycles in a season. I find *Orlaya grandiflora* is particularly good at this, as long as I do not collect the seed too efficiently in spring.

» The best advice I can give anyone about dressing a table is that you need fewer flowers than you think. Tables are for eating and drinking as well as looking lovely, and plates and bottles and knives and forks and glasses take up a lot of space. And candlesticks – it is not an event without candles.

Knocking over the flowers is poor form and means rivulets of water on people's knees. If you want to go for urns and jugs, and you really do think your table is wide enough, then feel free – as long as you bear in mind that these shouldn't come higher than your guests' chins when seated. Anything taller (except the lightest of wisps) will get in the way of sparkling conversation and someone, probably my mother, will pointedly take the arrangement off the table and put it on the floor.

»If you did the planning as described in chapter II, this moment will be a dream. Take a few round, focal flowers for the drama. This is probably the moment to take the scissors to your best David Austin. Be sure to put them in wide-bottomed, heavy glass bottles, otherwise they simply topple over. Add some foliage as a backdrop, the fillers, scented and fresh. Dill maybe, or mint. Then come the special bits. The wild strawberries, deep-brown cherry tomatoes. Don't skimp – don't just add a stem of sweet pea, get the vine and the tendril in there.

a living space

As much as I adore a party, my favourite meal is breakfast the next day. It
is always special, the morning after the night before. Guests emerge sleepily
into the dew from the tent in the corner of the orchard and I brew coffee
on the camp stove. They watch the sun come round the hill and eat toast
surrounded by flowers. It never fails to charm, and other people's joy in what
is an everyday experience for me is a fresh reminder of what a garden can do
for the soul. Why do I forget so often?

Because I find it so much easier to be in motion, to be doing, to be growing.
Unless I intentionally craft the space with places for sitting, for rest, then I
just won't. To just take in the beauty of the space, the edge of the hill, the
light on the trees, the hum of the bees in the flowers on a midsummer's day,
I need a place to sit.

I don't think I am overstating it when I say that a hammock changed our
lives. We waited until the great white cherry and the quince were big enough
to hold the ends; looking up at the swelling quinces only adds to the luxury.
A mid-afternoon iced coffee under a fruit tree in late summer can truly make
life worth living.

Once I learned the lesson of the hammock, I applied it in all sorts of ways.
A short plank on the ends of green oak blocks leaning against the house,
facing east for the morning light at breakfast. The camping table and chairs
pressed into service for a cup of tea after lunch by the meadow. Benches and
tables by the firepit for evening picnic suppers. A corkscrew and candlesticks
stashed down the side of the compost heap. The field is to the east of the
cottage and the sun sets on the other side of the thatch, behind some
ancient and huge lime trees, meaning the light drops early in the evening.
Blankets and jumpers or a big fire are needed by sundown even in the
height of summer.

jobs for late summer

———————

HARVEST FLOWERS, ESPECIALLY DAHLIAS AND ROSES,
AND COMBINE WITH HERBS, FRUITING BRANCHES AND
VEGETABLES IN URNS AND VASES IN THE HOUSE

KEEP CUTTING SWEET PEAS AND COSMOS

START TO COLLECT SEED FROM FLOWERS
WITH RIPENED SEED HEADS

WATER

WEED

RELAX

ENJOY

———————

V.
EARLY AUTUMN:
ABUNDANCE & HARVEST

SEPTEMBER

SATURDAY 5

I wake early and find the season has changed.
The air is cooler but the light is warmer. It
streams through the windows and I take
terrible grainy dark photos. Lunch out, and
then I drive home west into the low sun.

MONDAY 7

On my way to Torquay, I turn left through
the village and go up the hill. The Blackdowns
are flat on the top and steep on the sides.
The weather is always different at the top
and bottom, and sure enough, there is mist
rolling across the road at the junction for
Churchinford. The beeches form a tunnel.
One of them, just one, has turned a shocking
yellow. The first to turn.

THURSDAY 10

Harvesting corn on the cob. There are gaps
appearing in the kitchen garden and in the
cutting beds. The flowers are smaller now,
although there is a sense of endurance about
them. Things take longer to go over at this time
of year. I stop cutting the cosmos and let the
seed fall. Although it is technically not hardy,
I know there will be seedlings in spring.

FRIDAY 11

The dog walks take longer and longer. Hugo
picks blackberries along the lane and catches
his ears in the thorny cables. Maud chases mice
in and out of the long grass and refuses to be
dissuaded. I stop and check them for burdocks
stuck in their feathers and in their tails.

The dogs have fully embraced the change in
the season and there are beds strewn all over
the house, covered in snoring setters. Morag
has her own chair. For me, though, it has been
a busy week. As much as the year should be
slowing down, and everything should be stews
and woollen socks and sofas, there is a sense
of rushing to get everything done before it is
too late, and I'll be honest, I can't fit it all in.
The weather is positively filthy. The days are
shortening rapidly. However, the vegetable
plugs are almost all planted in their final beds.
The hardy annuals are all sown. Autumn is
the time to be sowing meadows.

THURSDAY 17

I am planning a dyeing garden. I sit all day
outside a courtroom on a hard bench and lose
myself in the magic of adding rusty nails to
the dye pot, the unpredictable serendipity of
yellows from lady's bedstraw, and the ancient
names of woads, welds and dyer's tickseed.

FRIDAY 18

Rain. Rain and rain and rain. Wet dogs and the
dahlias have mildew. But the cafe au laits have
started to curl and twirl from the centre, which
is one of the most beautiful things ever.

SATURDAY 19

A slower morning of soup and studio time.
Packing orders and prepping boxes. The house
is starting to fill up with boxes; boxes of seeds,
boxes of envelopes, even boxes of boxes for the
Christmas hampers. More boxes of hand-dyed
silk ribbon arrive.

MONDAY 21

Stormy weather. I brave some time in the
kitchen garden and pull out the last of the
tomatoes before I am driven in by the rain.
We abandon any idea of work for the evening
and go for supper at The Lyme Bay café. The
wind howls and the rain is horizontal. It is so
dark that it isn't possible to see the sea even
from close, but the waves can be felt. We sit by
the kitchen in the light and warmth and feel
glad to be safe.

TUESDAY 22

Tomatoes. The red ones are eaten with
mozzarella brought back from Italy. The green
ones are put in a bowl with a banana, covered
with a cloth, then put on a high shelf because
Maud eyes them with interest. (Putting them
on the windowsill will give tasteless tomatoes
with tough skins. Bananas and darkness are
much better.)

WEDNESDAY 23

A day of compost. We now have three bays of compost. The first has four squash plants in. The second is six-month-old compost curing, and the third is being filled. The third was starting to overflow and I kept just throwing things on top (if you are in a mild area and cut back your scabious, you might get one last flush, hence my compost heap being full of scabious stalks). Compost needs little attention day to day, but every so often, it does need some physical effort and a turn.

THURSDAY 24

The apples are falling from the trees with regular thuds. I pick the pears before they fall as the tree is in a container in the courtyard and I don't want them to bruise. Two catch me out by being the shell of a pear skin but full of wasps rather than fruit. I planted two damson trees last year (our Shropshire Prune proved to be a martyr to leaf curl aphid). I did not think they would have fruited yet and I was wondering how I would make pickled damsons.

SATURDAY 26

There is a scent in the air. Dahlias don't really smell, although dried ones do, oddly. It takes me all day to work out what it is. Quinces. A last ditch attempt to ripen them on a sunny windowsill has proven more successful than I ever could have hoped. I keep catching wafts of the most beautiful flowery notes.

SUNDAY 27

It feels like a day for tidying. I am not a tidy person, but a few hours here and there at this time of year can mean the world over the winter. So I trim hedges. The beech, the hedge germander between the kitchen garden beds. To be fair, these have needed trimming for a while and the hedges have been getting floppier and the beds smaller. I find a row of beetroot I'd forgotten about under the spent flower spikes.

MONDAY 28

The sky is as clear as cornflowers and the sun blazing hot. There are some changes afoot. I lift some Mypex that had been bringing part of the wilder end of things into beautiful no-dig production. I am very, very disappointed to discover quite a lot of very white thistles and an entire web of bindweed roots. I spread compost over it and put the Mypex back. I had been planning to plant it up with whitecurrants and loganberries but that will have to wait.

cutting and conditioning: how and when

I may have to break this to you gently, but your fantasies of cutting flowers in a floaty linen dress and laying them in a wicker trug? Not true. You can harvest tomatoes like this if you wish, even runner beans or beetroot if you must, but not flowers. First, you need to be up and out in the cool of the day (if this proves impossible in the long days of high summer, maybe the cool of the evening, but never in the heat of the day), and second, you need to cut into water.

As with trowels and hoes, you will end up with a favourite bucket. I personally find the robust ones with handles on the side the best. I know some people swear by loop handles, so they can put them over their arm, but I invariably end up putting the stems on the wrong side of the handle, which then squashes everything when I lift up the bucket. They do need to be rigid enough not to crack around the lip. Water can be surprisingly heavy and if you pick up a bucket by its edge, it can bow. You may need to pay a bit extra for a sturdy one, but it will last.

I have taps for water in both the kitchen garden and the field, which makes life easier, but if you have to carry lots of flowers and their containers, I would strongly recommend a garden trolley. A flat wheelbarrow on four wheels, it's practical and easy to manoeuvre, and stops the water from sploshing everywhere. If you know it's going to be hot on the day you harvest, it's worth preparing ahead. Rinse out your buckets and half-fill them with water.

I always take a bucket and a trug with me. Each time I cut a stem, I strip the lower leaves off into the trug and then drop the stripped stem into the bucket of water. How many of the leaves you strip off is a matter of taste, but any leaves below the waterline will rot and that reduces the vase life of the flowers significantly.

Cut when the flowers are just starting to come out. Roses are best cut when the sepals have just turned back. Cosmos when one single petal has turned out. Peonies when their buds are soft but not yet unfurled. Foxgloves, delphiniums and lupins when about a third of the flowers are open and two thirds are still in bud. The exception is dahlias, which do have to be open. Fading or 'over' flowers will not last in the vase any better than they will on the plant so I may as well do some deadheading and tidying up while I am there. These go straight into the trug. Dahlias and roses particularly benefit from you keeping on top of this.

Flowers cut at their very best first thing in the morning. If the dew is heavy or it is raining, you can still cut, but make sure the flowers aren't packed tight into the buckets, they'll need a bit of air around them to dry off. I have found two exceptions to this. Borage flops dreadfully early in the season, but you can increase your chances of it drinking by cutting it last thing at night and then leaving it in a deep bucket of water outdoors in the cool. This also works with lilac, especially if you cut the stem at a very sharp angle.

Flowers then need a rest and a drink. Anywhere cool, airy and dark is perfect. Think of how you would dry your washing on a washing line, and do the opposite. Keep out of sunshine, and out of breezes. If you cut in the morning, then a daytime rest is enough. If you need to cut in the cool of the evening, leave them overnight.

Some flowers, most notably poppies, benefit from a dip in hot water, straight out of the kettle, before going back into deep cool water. This really is the only way to get Icelandic poppies to go more than a day and even then, you need to cut them just as they are opening.

Once you have got your flowers in the house, many of the same principles apply. Keep them cool and out of direct sunlight and change the water religiously every day.

I must say, all of this only matters if you really care about it, and if longevity is what you want from flowers. If you have offered to do your best friend's wedding, or have a party and you need to impress, then take this terribly seriously. Most of the time, I don't. I have a garden full of flowers and a tiny cottage, so if my roses shatter all over the kitchen table after a day and a half, I'm fine with that. If the chicory is looking particularly fine, I'll cut it down and drag it up the stairs and put it in a pickling jar by the bed. My windowsills are covered in little pots, jars and bottles of dried sticks and twigs, poppy-seed heads, dried strawflowers and shots of electric-blue dried cornflowers. I'm not sure I am all that keen on everything looking fresh and pert and lovely anyway. Life isn't really like that.

creating a seasonal bouquet

YOU WILL NEED
» **7 stems flowers**

» **7 stems foliage**

» **7 seedheads stems or fruits**

» **String or garden twine**

» **Brown paper**

You've put all the work in, and now it is time to reap the rewards. Even in a small courtyard garden, a few plants can produce a lot of flowers, especially if you keep cutting them. Now is the time to enjoy them. Now is the time to bring them into the house, or to give them to friends and loved ones.

» A seasonal bunch of flowers for giving away is such a joy, and easy to put together. Aim for around a third foliage, a third filler and a third flowers, and then add a few special bits. They don't all have to be the same filler or the same foliage because that will look very boring indeed, but I wouldn't go for all different things either. A bit of a variety if you can, but not every single stem different.

» You can put it together in your hand, but remember to takes the leaves off the stem because they really will get in the way otherwise. Lay out all your flowers and bits of greenery on a table in front of you, and take up the first one in your non-dominant hand. Use your other hand to pick up and add the different stems, alternating foliage, filler and flowers so everything doesn't clump together and come out lopsided. If you keep your hand holding the flowers quite relaxed, forming a circle with your fingers and thumb, you can act as if this is the neck of a vase and just keep dropping the flowers through the circle, letting the stems cross and support each other.

» If this feels a bit difficult, then use a jug or vase with a narrow neck and just keep adding your foliage, fillers and flowers to it until you are happy with it. You will need to trim the stems so that all the flowers sit at roughly the same level to do it this way. Once everything is in, tie a piece of string around the neck of the vase or jug and tighten it all up. You can then take the flowers out of the vase, and you will have a hand-tied bouquet.

» Wrap the bouquet using brown paper to make it look really professional. If you are travelling any distance with it, take the vase with you and make sure the bouquet is in water until you hand it over, if you possibly can.

» There are many weeks that go by when I do not make a full bouquet, even in the height of summer. Flowers for my own pleasure are much more likely to be simple, single variety arrangements. A bud vase full of sweet peas next to the bed, filling the room with scent. A mug with a rose in it because I haven't got round to finding a proper container. An old ink bottle with grasses and seed heads in the old, tiny window half way up the stairs.

the wonder of seeds

I appreciate I am a little biased, but this is where the absolute magic of growing happens. I can just about get my mind around how utterly incredible it is that you can take a speck of matter, sometimes barely bigger than a bit of dust, and then it turns into a plant. Sometimes a huge plant. Maybe even a tree. I can just about grasp the wonder of that. But the fact that once you have a plant, that it will likely produce hundreds, maybe thousands of those little specks, every single one of them ready to give you a whole new plant – that is just too wonderful.

All gardening is just piggy-backing on what nature does without us. I never feel this more than when I am collecting seed. However different the seed, the process is generally the same. The flower is fertilized, the seed forms and ripens, and is dispersed. Although the method of dispersion varies – and I have ruined more woolly jumpers with *Daucus carota* and Cynoglossum seed, which are rough and designed to catch on to passing animals, than I care to think about – the intent is to get the ripe seed from the plant and on to fertile and receptive ground. Even as a grown-up, I have never got out of the habit of pulling ripe grass seed heads and tossing them into the air.

The closer what you do is to the natural process, the easier you are going to make things for the plant and for yourself. You'll never get a better carpet of perfect, healthy seedlings than by taking a flower that has set seed and started to drop them, and shaking it enthusiastically over a freshly hoed flower bed.

Of course, we gardeners want to spread the seed so it grows in specific places. So that the species foxgloves that have flowered all summer long might look lovely in a trough by the front door. Or so that the briza grass that has flourished along the edge of the studio might look perfect dappled between chocolate cosmos. We might also want it to grow at specific times. Many of the plants that can grow and prosper in our mild springs and summers cannot endure our cold wet winters. My cosmos, a half-hardy annual, produces buckets and buckets of blooms and, if left, sacks and sacks of shiny, dark, curved seed. But if I let this fall and grow where it stands, the seedlings will not make it through to spring. I need to keep the seed cool and dry – that is, dormant – until conditions are just right.

As with fruit, what I want is ripeness. Seed collected when it is not quite ready may continue to develop once you have cut it, but it may not. Generally, I'm looking for a change in texture and a change in colour. The green swellings that form behind the flower start to dry to a caramel brown, and then the cracks start to appear. For foxgloves, the seams split down the sides, a little at first, and then they go with a rent, like bending over in splitting trousers. For poppies, tiny vents appear beneath the flat crown. Nigella starts to open at the top, all the better for collecting; if I get them at the right moment, I can cut and tip them upside down into a paper bag without spilling a single precious one.

This is always the challenge of seed collecting: too early and they aren't ready and I have to use my nails to open the seed head to try to get them out; too late and I can turn the seed head upside down to find it is nothing but an empty husk, the contents having sprinkled or flown or dropped before I was able to catch them. Signs to look for are rattling seed, papery husks, or a tiny split in the edge of the casing.

If this is all sounding a bit too good to be true, there are a few snags. To understand the hows and wherefores, you need to get your head round a few things. These mainly relate to how plants are bred, or crossed, to give us the varieties that we know.

OPEN-POLLINATED SEEDS

These are plants and flowers that are pollinated by wildlife and wind. Although humans have been selecting what seeds are saved and grown on over hundreds of years, this is something that has occurred slowly and been more about choosing the best plants to collect seed from, rather than intervening in how the seed is set. I grow a lot of wild carrot in my field. It can reach about 1.2m (4ft), sometimes taller, in my very fertile soil. It always has insects on it and, once it has set seed, I am always picking the toothy seeds off my clothes and flicking them off, distributing them around and about. They grow where they fall. Sometimes they drift into the field next door, creating dots of white in the green pasture. No one owns *Daucus carota*, it just is. If you sow a *Daucus carota* seed, you will get a *Daucus carota* plant. That is, it comes 'true'.

So why on earth would a plant produce a seed that didn't produce a plant that looked like its parent? When it is an F1. This is when a selected plant is pollinated (usually mechanically) with the pollen from another variety of the same species. The seed from this plant, the first generation of the cross pollination, is called a hybrid. Hybrids are usually selected and carefully bred for certain qualities. These are normally the ones that suit commercial production: straight stems, blight resistance, vigour and very specific colours. If you buy hybrids and sow them and grow them, the plants around them of the same species will start to pollinate and cross with them, and they will change and shift in their qualities and habits; their seeds will not come 'true'. The features that you bought the seed for will only last a generation, and then you have to buy more.

composting

For many, compost has come to be the stuff that comes in a bag from the garden centre in the same way that bread is the stuff that comes in a bag from the supermarket. Just like bread, compost offers varying degrees of nutrition – and there is nothing like the version you make at home. This is for many reasons: you know what has gone into it, you know its lifecycle and its temperatures, you know its journey. As with making bread, creating beautiful compost is a skill that takes time to develop but is well worth the investment.

There are many different ways of approaching compost and I've tried a wide range. Many of these have been a failure and it is only recently that I have struck upon a recipe that suits me and my field. I think compost-making is a difficult skill to learn by reading about it alone. Like baking bread, it is a physical and tactile process, reliant almost entirely on an appreciation of texture.

Almost anything that you have cut, mown or weeded out of your garden can be composted, as well as much of the food waste from your kitchen. Anything plant-based that will decompose is good for your compost heap. But for really good compost, compost that heats up and turns even the most unpromising weeds into brown, crumbly life-filled matter, it is worth paying attention to the mix of materials. Old gardening hands talk so casually of ratios of green and brown, but for me it has taken years to fully understand. In essence, you are going to need a lot more green than you think, and if you leave greens composted for any length of time, they become browns.

This is not to say that if you just pile everything you have in a heap, you will not eventually get compost. You will, but it will probably take an incredibly long time. Small gardens and courtyard gardens rarely have the space to tie up to such a commitment and I, for one, am really not that patient. Until I was in the position to devote a corner of the orchard to compost bays, the vast majority of my weeds and branches went to my local recycling centre, and I brought it back in bags of organic matter for winter top-dressing. It was only easy, quick-to-break-down flowers from the fields, and roots and leaves from the kitchen garden that went into my compost-making. Plus mown grass. If you want to make compost really quickly, mown grass is perfect.

WHAT TO ADD

Mown grass is your ultimate green. It is very high in nitrogen although you can't really tell that from looking at it. What you can tell is that when chopped finely it feels quite moist to the touch, and rots incredibly quickly. A pile of grass clippings can get too hot to touch in a few days if it is kept damp. For compost-making, this is rocket fuel.

Other greens include:
» Vegetable leaves and kitchen waste, anything you pull off when you are preparing vegetables from the garden
» Tea bags
» Deadheaded flowers, or flowers that are over and you are pulling out
» Green, sappy weeds
» Farmyard manure

Although greens are generally quite soft, cutting them up and increasing their surface area will speed up the rate of decomposition and get your compost to its final stage more quickly. But you cannot make good compost with greens alone. They will collapse into themselves, turn into slime, and then sort of just disappear.

Which leads us to browns. The greens start the decomposition process going, but what gives your compost body are the dry bits of organic matter mixed in with them. The combination of the two is what creates the magic process of composting. I get a lot of cardboard through my business, and this makes a perfect brown. Not because it is brown, but because it is quite dry and fibrous. As with greens, the greater the surface area, the faster the rate of decomposition. That's why I tear the boxes up before mixing them in to the greens. I've also recently got hold of a shredder to chop up the branches and other woody waste that comes from the field, which has proved revolutionary in terms of how fast the heap heats up and breaks down.

Other browns include:
» Sawdust
» Paper
» Autumn leaves
» Straw or hay
» Wood or bark chippings
» Egg boxes

Some things to avoid:
I don't put any shiny printed boxes in because of the amount of ink. Similarly, junk mail or those shiny leaflets go in the recycling box, not the compost heap. The other thing to avoid, perhaps surprisingly, is coffee grounds. We get through a lot of coffee in our house and conventional wisdom is that it is a great source of nitrogen and micronutrients. But it's also a great source of caffeine, which is a toxin released by the coffee plant to reduce competition from the plants around it. (A thank you to botanist James Wong for that knowledge.) That's right, putting coffee grounds on your beds actively reduces their vigour and, in enough quantities, kills them. I admit I do still put some in the big compost heaps because, even with my coffee habit, the grounds make up only a fraction of the greens I include. But if you are composting in the barrel-style bins or on a very small scale, be mindful.

I have vole tunnels all over my orchard, and I know there are mice in the greenhouse because they take the tips of my marigolds. But I do not, as far as I know, have rats. To avoid them getting in your compost heap, don't add cooked food waste, meat or dairy. If you do get rats in your compost, however, don't panic. I have heard they are excellent for aerating and turning a heap. They might also be a sign that the heap is a bit dry. Compost that is decomposing fast is quite hot and moist and not a very attractive place for mammals to live. Try adding more greens, giving it a good stir and then watering well. I have no suggestions about how to get rid of voles. I have long resigned myself to co-habitation.

MY ROUTINE FOR COMPOST-MAKING

I think you need at least two bays or compost bins, but ideally three. If you do only have one, be extra vigilant with getting the ratio of greens and browns right and ideally make sure it's one with a detachable side, so you can really turn your compost well.

The aim of compost-making is not only to get the material to break down as fast as possible and get it to a state where you can spread it on your beds, but also to create something that is rich, vibrant and microbially alive. To achieve this, you need to understand how to create the conditions for microbes to thrive, and to introduce the bacteria and bugs that are perfectly suited to your growing space – the indigenous microorganisms (IMOs) that belong to your garden and your garden only.

Your compost heap should always be sat on soil, directly on the ground, not only to allow excess water to drain, but also to allow IMOs and bacteria to get into the decomposing materials. These are already present in the soil, so putting your compost heap in contact with the earth will help them move in quickly and easily. Placing your compost heap on a particularly rich area of IMO life is even better. My bays are tucked into a hedge in a corner, a site both out of the way and easily accessible. It was serendipity that this was also the ideal place for inoculation. Areas where leaves fall and rot are teeming with IMOs – just think how rich woodland soil is.

If it isn't possible to put your compost heap in such a place, simply put a few trowels of earth from your garden into the base of your heap before you start building, or make a pot of LAB (see page 95) to inoculate it with – the gardening equivalent of a sourdough starter. I have also had incredible results from adding biodynamic preparations.

As you weed or cut flowers, start to spread them across in the bottom of the heap. I find it useful to have a little pile of damp cardboard next to the heap so I can layer as I go along. I use the word 'layer' cautiously – there needs to be a bit of mixing going on, too. If you build your heap like a lasagne with sheets of cardboard or barriers of thick brown branches between the layers, then the reactions and the decomposition just never get going. So, some green bits, some brown bits. A 50:50 ratio between the two is best and a little stir as you go along doesn't hurt, either; you're aiming to keep it loose and light so there is air in the mixture too.

The one thing that changed my compost-making was a shredder. Turning a compost heap filled with branches and long stems is unsatisfying and difficult, and the smaller surface areas mean decomposition takes a long time. Putting everything through a chipper accelerates the process and means you aren't pulling sticks out of your fine finished compost. A decent one is quite an investment, though, which is why it took me about ten years to get round to buying one. If anyone suggests you run a lawnmower over twiggy brown bits to break them down, don't believe them. It doesn't work.

Most people, me included, take quite some time to fill up a whole compost heap, which is why it is useful to have two. One that is being built and added to, and one that is cooking. Every so often, pour a watering-can's worth of water over them. You will know when you have your green/brown/water recipe exactly right because your heap will radiate heat fast. When I first got this right and my temperature probe showed 65°C (150°F), I could not have been more proud of myself. I checked the temperature on an almost hourly basis. And then I turned the compost and accidentally buried the thermometer, never to be seen again, so now I just have to stick my hand in. If it feels warm under the top layer, I'm happy.

TURNING THE COMPOST HEAP

I am intrinsically lazy when it comes to hard physical labour and I always
put this task off for as long as possible. But the reality is significantly less
arduous than the anticipation. If I tackle it first thing, my air of satisfaction
lasts the whole day. There are ways of turning your heap without taking
the whole thing out, such as by using a sort of corkscrew-type auger, but I
have never found these effective. The time to turn is about six weeks after
your greens-and-browns mix has reached the top of the bay (it will sink
alarmingly, so this might take longer than you think) and the heap has built
up some good heat. Turning does two things: it reduces the temperature,
preventing the compost from getting so hot that it kills the beneficial
microorganisms, and it introduces air, so the process of decomposition
can continue. Yes, like stretching and folding sourdough.

If I have a spare bay, I will turn into this, but more often I lay a tarpaulin
out next to the heap and just dig out the layers. Once it is all out on the
tarpaulin, I have a check through for any dry bits – branches that are
too thick or woody to break down, or any lumps that need distributing.
Sometimes bits of cardboard stick together and need a bit of shaking out.
If this is a really hard physical task, your heap is probably too wet; it should
be fluffy rather than claggy. Sometimes my bottom layers are not composting
at all and almost preserved. This means these patches are too dry. Once it is
a bit more mixed, put it back in the heap, making sure you spread it evenly
across the bay. Once everything is back in, give it a water again, and then
leave to mature.

jobs for early autumn

SOW HARDY ANNUALS SEEDS FOR NEXT YEAR

COLLECT SEEDS

KEEP HARVESTING DAHLIAS

TAKE PHOTOGRAPHS OF PLANTS THAT YOU HAVE
PARTICULARLY LIKED, OR COMBINATIONS THAT
HAVE WORKED WELL

TRIM HEDGES AND EDGES

VI.
LATE AUTUMN & EARLY WINTER:
REST & RESTORE

OCTOBER

THURSDAY 1

I may have fully embraced the change in the
season, but the flowers bloom on. The roses
are having a last hurrah. The Helianthus is
smothered in bees. (I detest the colour but I
cannot bring myself to deprive them of it by
digging it out.) The cornflowers go on and
on and on.

FRIDAY 2

A hurricane is forecast and I cut what I can.
I am trying to dry lots of things for Christmas
wreaths, but the rain keeps everything damp
before I have a chance to cut it. The colours
seem to intensify every day.

SATURDAY 3

The spaniel has a haircut to prepare us for the
season of mud. The house is full of daddy-
longlegs and the field is full of puddles and
drips. I feel like we may have missed the sharp,
crisp, bright autumn days and slid straight into
winter. I harvest the strawflowers that have
gone over and push out their seeds with my
thumb. The side buds, where the flowers have
not fully opened to show the yellow centre, are
wired and laid out to dry.

WEDNESDAY 7

This week has been mostly about the rain. I had
hoped to experiment with drying dahlias and
grasses. It has simply not stopped raining for
long enough.

THURSDAY 8

My seed business is on the up. People in
London wanted to talk to me about things.
I was born in London. I spent some of the
finest years of my life there. I was so excited to
be going there, to arrive there, and within two
hours of being there, I was ready to be back in
the country. I soothe myself with endless coffees
and photographing words on shop-fronts.

FRIDAY 9

Back to reality. Everything is heavy in the rain.
Blooms, full of water. Droplets sit on leaves
and petals. I wonder if city life would be so
bad after all.

SATURDAY 10

Another city. This time Bristol. A wonderful
day of learning and chatting and catching up.
Home to packing sweet peas. Piggy sue is going
out in fat envelopes. There is officially a run on
them and my inbox is full of people desperate
to get their hands on the precious packets.

SUNDAY 11

Mushrooms start to appear everywhere I look. The smell of autumn has not arrived yet, but there are signs. I roast squash with the seeds from the bolted fennel. I light candles in the shortening evenings.

Much of the first part of the week was spent avoiding the rain. Huddling in the house until the last minute, watching the dampness hanging in the air and dripping inexorably off the thatch. There is a greyness in the days that is infectious; it seeps into my bones and I feel limp. We order firewood and put trays of vegetables and thyme in the top oven for soups and stews. Pots of stock simmer in the bottom oven, fighting the gloom with a scent of nourishing comfort. The kettle is boiled over and over again as I brace myself to go out with the dogs, or to pull leeks from the back corner of the house garden, for trips to the post office with dyer's bundles and brass wreath hoops. It feels like it will never end. That it will never be dry again, and the sun will never shine. I feel cheated of the autumn that I longed for. Instead of tweed and scarves and fingerless mittens, we seem to be lost in a wet cloud of leaky wellingtons, clammy Barbours and damp, gritty dogs.

SATURDAY 17

And then just like that, it passed. The sky turned a crisp and sharp blue. The sun set in a blaze of delight. The rose hips glistened in the fresh new light. And for the sheer exuberance of delight that the season was redeemed, I set off for Bailey's Home in Ross on Wye.

SUNDAY 18

A dry day. The sun is warm and it is as if the rain has never been. We walk and the girls chase pheasants with joyous abandon. I weed as much of the kitchen garden as I can in the time I have. I harvest the remaining huge pumpkins, slapping them gently to check they sound hollow. They are put in the greenhouse. I wish they had had longer in the sun, but as there has been no sun to be had, there seems little point leaving them to get cold as the weather turns. The cornflowers have been flowering since the spring and are starting to look tired. I cut the last perfect ones for pressing and let the rest go. The dahlias are also tired and have mildew. Blooms that are just coming out and haven't yet started to turn their petals back are put in the trolley and brought into the house for hanging and drying. Roses are having a second flush and those still in bud are taken, too. Hydrangeas are poached from my mother's tiny walled garden. I run out of hooks and walls for hanging.

152

THURSDAY 22

This pumpkin was growing up the estate
fencing underneath the Bramley apple tree.
Every time I inspected it, which was often, it
threatened to topple and fall. Today, I take a
deep breath and cut it. I hate doing this because
unless you are really, really careful, it is all too
easy to cut a vine and cut off a smaller fruit
further along that really needed a bit more
growing time. But it is October now, and I
cannot imagine more growing will be done
this year. Not even any real ripening. I think
we may have had the last of the sunshine.

FRIDAY 23

It rains some more. I light the fire and eat
more stewed apple and quince than is probably
healthy. No gardening jobs were done at all
this weekend. If you did anything meaningful
outside this weekend, I salute you.

SUNDAY 25

Blue skies, and then rain, and then blue skies
again. Boots, coats, jumpers on and jumpers
off. It's not cold enough to light the fire but it
is grim enough to fill the table with candles.

MONDAY 26

This time of year, where the day length is the
same as the fast-growing part of spring, leads
to some funny things. There is blossom on
the apple trees. A fresh flush of *Daucus carota*,
borage in the meadow. The autumn-flowering
cherry, a very happy tree which brings a rare
flash of colour in the grimmest of months, has
both blossom and leaves.

WEDNESDAY 28

The Virginia creepers seem to be on fire.
There is one outside my cottage and another
outside my office window at work. Every time
I look up, there is scarlet. The liquidambers
(the strangest name for a tree) are curling and
colouring. One single beech in the churchyard
has turned the colour of butter. It won't be long
now and I will fill my house with branches of
mottled gold.

reflecting on the season

The ground is turning in on itself. The perennials sink back into the soil, leaving dried skeletons. The annuals are stalks, with the odd pop of muted colour. This is the point where any photographs you have taken throughout the year are invaluable. This is the time to view and review.

Did your garden do what you wanted it to do? For me, this shifts and changes season by season, month by month. Do I want to grow flowers for the sake of flowers? Do I want to grow enough food to sustain me and my family so I never have to go to the supermarket again? To provide much-needed respite for wildlife? To compost enough to create a carbon sink? Should I be gardening at all? Maybe I should just let it all revert to an untouched wilderness. And then I come back round to flowers. But with a touch of wild, of course.

Purists may disagree, but there is a point of garden management that falls on the side of wild but is far from manicured. This is where I am aiming. Romantic. Lush. Casually, recklessly, gloriously beautiful. You may be going for a more managed look. Maybe less. But this is the time of year when you can have a look at how you did, and what you might want to do differently next season.

'It will look better next year.' The gardener's lament. A refrain I am so guilty of uttering. While mature and bedded-in gardens often look more comfortable and peaceful, I tinker so much with my structure and outlines, my intentions and aims, that I rarely get to this stage. Or at least, I rarely feel like I get to this stage. But when I look at photographs taken when we dug out the trees, when my garden was still a field and sheep still grazed, I can see how far we have come. Even from last year, the fruit trees are a little thicker and more pleasing in their shape, the studio a little more smothered in the white floribunda rose that never had a name, the peonies so much stronger. Every year, the field feels more different and yet more connected to the landscape around it.

And so, as the weather cools and the seed catalogues appear, take the time to reflect. Which bits of your space did you enjoy the most? Which gladdened your heart? Where did you find your feet straying with a cup of tea? What looked good when? Lots of gardens can look good in June. A bit of wasteland next to a railway line will look good in June – the credit is not yours, it belongs only to nature. So what looked good once that flush of summer enthusiasm was over? What combinations of colours and textures stirred you? What turned out to be entirely the wrong height and habit for its space? I remembered again that I loathe sugar-pink tulips. I need to be reminded of this every few years when I have relented in my rules and slipped a few Albert Heijn into a planting scheme.

Annuals are so easily refreshed that it is easy to swipe a whole bed or border aside and start again. That is part of the joy of them, they are so easy come and easy go. Swap a white nigella out for a mix of pinks next year and you have a whole other look. Add grasses for a more meadowy look. Add French marigolds or a coreopsis for a bit of bold. With annuals from seed, the world really is your oyster for about the same price as a cup of coffee.

It is easy to get carried away with the seed catalogues, mind, so be a bit selective. Think about what has grown well and find other things that might suit a similar soil or aspect. Keep your choices coherent in terms of something (either height or colour) and make sure you think about the mix of textures and structural elements. Once you have finished curating, throw in two things that are completely new and different and wild and just catch your eye.

the bare-root season

The more permanent things, the trees and shrubs, the roses and the climbers, are not so amenable to whim. I think the problem is less that you might regret buying a plant, but that you regret not. With that in mind, a cautionary tale. I bought a beautiful *Cotinus* sapling a few years ago. I planted it entirely in the wrong place, in the middle of a bed that was intended for cutting. It looked in the wrong place, it grew in the wrong way, it shaded out some plants and was choked by others. In a late autumn review a few years ago, I chopped it down and dug it out. I don't look at the gap where it was and miss the tree, but I do look at the astonishing smoke-like flowers on a mature tree in the next village and regret my certainty. The moral of the story is to be a bit more careful with the placing of the bigger things.

But it is the bigger plants that make a garden look finished, that give it structure and style, atmosphere and feeling. Autumn is the time when you can source bare-root plants. These are plants that are grown in open ground (fields) and then dug up and sold without soil on in their dormant state. Not only do they grow on better than a plant that has been confined to a pot, but they are cheaper, too. Roses, fruit trees and hedging plants are all good investments.

Roses

My favourite roses for training over rose domes:
*The old roses are best, climbers. They don't cut brilliantly
but are beautiful in among softer planting.*
» **William Lobb**
» **Madame Plantier**
» **Comte de Chambord**

———

For cutting:
*Few garden roses last a long time in the vase, but they make up
for this with scent, and seductive and abandoned beauty.*
» **Crown Princess Margareta**
» **Sally Holmes** (single)
» **Jude the Obscure**

———

For clambering over walls and fences:
If you keep tying in and training them, they'll keep growing up.
» **Madame Alfred Carrière**
» **Generous Gardener**
» **Gloire de Dijon**

———

Rosa spinosissima gets a special mention because the hips are just incredible.
Purple/black. Wonderful.

≈ A David Austin variety, *Rosa* 'Grace'

feed the soil

Autumn, when the air is cold but the ground not yet hard underfoot, is the perfect time for getting some of that beautiful compost on to the beds. You might be winding down and heading for hibernation and wondering about putting the heating on, but the life in the soil is gearing up for the most important time in their yearly cycle. In autumn, leaves fall from trees and plants die back. The organic material sits layer upon layer over the soil, ready to be pulled deep into the ground and broken down by earthworms, micro-organisms and bacteria. There are times when the soil gives and gives, and this shift in the seasons is the time for it to take.

There is almost no such thing as too thick a layer of compost, but few of us have the luxury of such a thing. An 2.5cm (1 inch) spread as far as you can go will make all the difference in the world. Not only does this suppress the weeds, but it gives great heart to the soil underneath. Dark and crumbly compost should be full of life and nutrition and, at this time of the year, the ground should be free and empty. You just have to be careful around the stems and trunks of the bigger plants.

Years when I have had little of my own home-made compost, I have bought in trailer loads of recycled green waste which adds body, if not a lot of nutrition. That is, it is organic matter, but there is little microbial activity left in it after heat treatment and processing. In order to help get things going, I supplement with LAB (see page 95) but, in time, the indigenous microbes and funghi will incorporate it into the soil without your help. If you are laying compost on containers or very small beds, then a little can go a long way and a few bags of peat-free might be the simplest way.

Rudbeckia hirta 'Sahara'

tulip selection

If it matters to you when the first tulips arrive, and you want to be first out of the blocks with spring colour (only blossom really beats the first tulips), go for the earlies. Exactly when they will flower will depend on the weather: in March last year the field was under 12cm (5 inches) of snow and they were held back. Most seasons, the earlies will be solidly underway by April 1. The early tulips come in singles and doubles. Singles are the classic tulip shape, perfect goblets in rich shades. Doubles are more unusual, ruffles of layers, like a peony. Triumph tulips, a cross between the huge Darwin tulips and an early tulip, have classically egg-shaped blooms and strong, sturdy stems. This is the biggest group of tulips.

Rembrandt tulips are those beautiful streaked ones, so beloved of Dutch Masters, all rich, deep colours.

As there are almost as many tulips as there are colours, the choice can be overwhelming, although I believe less is more in terms of creating a harmonious palette. One of everything gives the visual effect of a bag of dolly mixtures, which I find too jumbly. Gardening guru Arthur Parkinson advises avoiding pink and sticking to the 'stained-glass' colours. Garden designer Arne Maynard created a combination called Burnt Toffee, which I have returned to again and again. It is the richness of tulips that I find so seductive, and it is the deep colours that do this best.

If you have only a small area in which to plant the winter bulbs, I think it is hard to beat a single variety for impact. White Parrot is intricate and dazzling. Queen of Night is strong and bold.

SINGLES

» *Apricot Beauty* (early)
» *Caravelle* (late)
» *Queen of the Night* (late)

———

DOUBLES

» *Brownie* (early)
» *Maureen* (late)

———

TRIUMPH

» *Havran*
» *Ronaldo*
» *Gabriella*
» *Cairo*
» *Disaronno*

———

REMBRANDT

» *Absalon*
» *Insulinde*

planting tulip bulbs

Bulbs have almost everything they need to grow so they are fairly straightforward. A few tips, though. Although some come back every year, you are better off treating tulips as annuals (if you want bulbs that keep coming back, try narcissi). But do rotate where you put them as the ground can develop problems such as tulip fire, a disease caused by the *Botrytis tulipae* fungus. You'll know it if you get it because your plants will appear scorched, with brown spots on the flowers and twisted, withered and distorted leaves. Planting them quite late in the season when the ground is really cold will help with this. But if you have had any problems growing tulips in the past, you might be better off putting them in pots. Add a bit of grit to the compost or the soil and plant much deeper than you think – about 20cm (8 inches).

When it comes to harvesting, tugging the whole stem up gets you a nice long flower for the vase, although it also makes the bulb less likely to bloom the next year. You can't have it all.

jobs for late autumn

————————

ORDER TULIP BULBS AND PLANT AFTER FIRST FROST

ORDER BARE-ROOT PLANTS

SPREAD COMPOST OVER THE TOPS OF POTS
AND FLOWER BEDS

CUT HYDRANGEAS FOR DRYING AND ROSE HIPS
FOR DECORATION

————————

VII.
WINTER:
CELEBRATE

DECEMBER

FRIDAY 4

A few weeks ago, on the path around the back field, we found the owl. There was a great sadness in finding it; its beauty undimmed in death, yet so still. Even the dogs stood back and looked at it, and then left it respectfully alone. As long as I have lived here, there has been an owl. Hooting in the woods that line Pickeridge Hill, living alongside the deer and the buzzards. The call is as familiar and as reassuringly regular as the ringing of the church bells next door. The silence has been a loud one. Today, though, we heard owls again. Someone once told me that the twit-twoo is in fact two owls – the call and the answer. The answer was a bit croaky, as if not quite yet used to public performing, not quite warmed up. It was a lovely sound. We walked late today, to listen to the owls, standing occasionally to hear them better. Bats followed us overhead. I thought they might just be late birds, but then they came so close the cut-out wings were clear. Like a child's drawing. Swooping.

Almost all dog walks are dark now. Sometimes we make this an adventure. We take torches to trudge over the fields, then sit at the base of the big oak trees and have hot stew out of bowls. There is a thermos of hot mulled cider, spiked with calvados. When we get home I make apple crumble. Tom Putt eater apples layered with Bramleys scrumped from next door. Spelt flour in the topping.

SATURDAY 5

The first proper hard frost. Finally. I hope for a cold crisp day, but the rain comes soon after. The dahlias look sad and the nasturtiums, which had been flowering prolifically, disappear overnight. The chimney sweep comes and brings gossip about things he has seen and heard while fitting woodburners. I light the fire. The dogs approve.

Dexter arrives. He is the biggest Irish setter I have ever seen, a distant relative of the girls. He is beautiful and young, which means he bounces around with no awareness of quite what he is doing. He spills coffee and breaks wine glasses. He tips over chairs. He gives cuddles that could break ribs and black eyes. He is gloriously goofy, maddening and adorable in equal measure. Hugo is utterly outraged at his arrival. Dexter doesn't notice. Maud takes to her bed in the kitchen and refuses to come out. It is impossible to stay cross with Dexter. It is also almost impossible to take his photograph because he wants to be standing on me the whole time, which makes it difficult to point a camera at him.

SUNDAY 6

There aren't many jobs to be done in the garden at this time, although keeping the paths clear of leaves will pay dividends. I find some perfect bulbs of Solent Wight garlic at the Trading Post Farm Shop in South Petherton and plant them in the rain.

FRIDAY 18

It rains with startling ferocity. The racecourse road is flooded. The water comes off the fields on the other side of the village, runs along the road, and is meant to turn down Mill Lane. But sometimes, when the storms are heavy, it turns too quickly, and heads towards our row of cottages. It is within inches of our front doors and we all paddle round in wellies, clearing drains so the water can flow past and away. When we go out with the dogs, it is absolutely wild. The girls splash through the deep puddles with joy and abandon. Hugo is slower than usual; he is at the fluffy state of his coat growth and soaks up mud and water like a mop. He is wrung out like a dishcloth before he is allowed in the house.

SATURDAY 19

Wreath time. Hampered by the weather. I was hoping for coppery gold wreaths in bracken and beech but everything except the most hardy conifers are sodden. Later-planted asparagus comes to the rescue, and lightens the heavy evergreen palette.

SUNDAY 20

The winter solstice. The shortest day. The longest night. It is dark so late this morning we wait patiently to walk, although it doesn't so much get light as get less dark. The streaks in the sky widen and turn to a blanket of pewter. The moon is the thinnest sliver. The human calendar is wrong. This is the moment the year turns.

MONDAY 21

Collected pine branches and cones, rose hips and asparagus, hazel twigs with the promise of buds. Wreaths for the village, and a final one for my own front door. Celebrate with smoked carrots on rye toast and mulled cider.

TUESDAY 22

Christmas guests arrive. I harvest leeks and kale from the kitchen garden for Christmas dinner. The eve is celebrated with our mothers, ricotta ravioli, a Potimarron squash and stilton pie, candles and the best napkins.

WEDNESDAY 23

Up to Otterford for an early morning walk. A light frost, we watch the sun rise with a flask of tea and a mince pie. Then a family walk. A child and a dog get stuck in the deep mud by the lake, both rescued by my brother and washed off in the stream. Christmas dinner. Endless champagne and Pipers Farm cheese.

THURSDAY 24

Fire lit and feet up. More cheese. Reading and writing.

inside & out

Now, more than ever, the boundary that keeps nature out of our homes is softened. Whole trees are welcomed into the sanctuary of our homes and drop needles on to carpets. Ivy is draped over pictures and mantelpieces as if growing up our walls. Holly is perched on Christmas puddings. We bring something precious inside; not the polite vases and blooms of high summer, but the wildness of forest-found branches, boughs and swags. The doors of our homes, the sites of our going out and coming in, are hung with circles of evergreens. On Christmas Eve, we walk back through the village rather than along the stream. The windows sparkle with dressed trees. Each door displays a wreath of rustic abundance or elegant refinery, both betraying the pagan roots of our knowledge of the unending circle of the seasons.

Flowers and colour are precious in these dark days and bulbs have to be forced out of their natural cycle to bloom in the depths of winter. Paper-white narcissi, amaryllis and hyacinths bring some floral colour, but they are hard-won and timing is all. They are too showy for me, and do not respect the plants' need for rest. Better I think to let luck and chance play its part and be grateful for what is freely given. A snow-white hellebore – *Helleborus niger*, the Christmas rose – blooms unexpectedly in the shaded trough by the back door, pushing through some tatty pennisetums and leaning on a box ball. My mother has a willow wreath that is many years old, which, despite being in a centrally heated house and hung on a wall with no natural light, puts out the most perfect silver furry buds, just in time for Christmas. I cannot help feeling that there is very old magic in willow.

on willow

Somerset is willow country. It grows here better than anywhere else, although it is generally a very forgiving tree and happy in many gardens, fields and hedges. I saw a picture of coloured willow once, a row of pencil-like rods in the most perfect tones of damson, silver, yellow, orange, sharp acid yellow. I determined that I would have a willow collection, one of each. After some searching, I found a source of willow in Bristol, and collected a precious bundle of different colour twigs from a terraced villa in Totterdown. Striking willow cuttings is not difficult; simply take a part of the willow stem about 20cm (8 inches) long and push it into soil just over halfway. The only thing that can possibly go wrong is that you get it upside down (check which way the buds are going, they point towards the tip), and even then, the indomitable willow will probably grow. My dream was that this perfect tapestry of willow colour would form the windbreak on the far side of my flower field, the east fence, parallel with the curve of the valley. The willow certainly took, and grew up and out with enthusiasm, although the more common varieties of pale, silvery greens and mustard yellow soon out-competed the more delicate colours. Within three years the line of plants was over 6m (20ft) tall, even though it was coppiced to the ground every winter to make multi-coloured woven wreaths for Christmas.

Someone once said that a weed is simply a plant in the wrong place. A row of enthusiastically growing trees in the wrong place is a problem. They were hauled out by hand last summer with immense trouble and effort, and replaced with a polite row of beech whips. I let the last two of my favourite colours stay, however, and it isn't winter until I have woven a few willow rings.

If you do not grow your own willow, it is prolific in hedges. Wild willow (aka goat willow or crack willow) will weave if you are patient and not fastidious, but rarely will it produce the smooth rope-like effect of cultivated willow. Also look out for little patches of black on the whip. This is canker and it will inevitably bend at these points of weakness. You can buy willow for weaving (check if it needs soaking first), but also ask around your local flower growers – many have one or two trees for supplying stems. If you have a dogwood or hazel, you can weave it in a similar way. However, I have spent so long weaving willow that other woods feel so foreign in my hands that it is like speaking French.

weaving a willow wreath

YOU WILL NEED

» **12 stems of coloured willow**

» **Strong secateurs**

» **2m of mixed ribbons**

» Choose your stems. Smooth, long, straight ones are the best. You may need to cut a little away from the bottom; willow stems are a bit like asparagus – the lowest bit can be too hard and brittle to be of much use. If you run your hand up, there will be a moment where it starts to feel more pliable and workable. Cut there.

» The number of stems you cut will determine the size of your final wreath. Most woven wreaths go through an awkward stage where they look a bit wonky and clumsy, and the only way of fixing them is to keep adding more stems. Make sure you have more rather than fewer stems, just in case. I'd start with about 12. It is generally better to go smaller and fatter than bigger and thinner, unless you are a dab hand.

» Check the stems for damage or canker. The rods will snap at these points easily and half the job of wreath-making is avoiding any kinks or corners in the willow. Smooth, soft curves is what you are after.

» Put some old trousers on and make a cup of tea. Willow weaving cannot be hurried, or done under stress. It is immensely meditative and satisfying (the clichés about its teaching basket weaving in high-security prisons have their roots in truth), but you need to be gentle and focused. Lay out your stems within easy reach and pick the longest. Do not try to force it to bend before you have softened its fibres. Starting at one end, gently rub it backwards and forwards across the front of your knee. This sounds very odd, but what you are aiming for is for the fibres that keep the willow upright to start to soften and become a gentle curve. After a few passes across your knee, you will feel the willow give, and when you hold it away from you, the rod will stay curved. Move the rod from one hand to the next, passing each section of it across your knee a few times, until the whole rod, from cut end to tip, is soft and pliable. Like a masseur finding a knot, you might find that some bits of the rod are more resistant than others.

≈ Soften the willow by running it across your knee

≈ Thread the end through the loop

» However, a bit of pressure will usually yield results. I find that doing this in a warm place means the willow is happier to bend, but that might be because I am happier to work it for longer if I am warm and comfortable. Patience and kind hands are key here.

» You can either soften all your rods at once, or as you go along. Take the longest rod and curve it into a circle roughly the size of the wreath you want. Smaller ones are easier to start with, but if you want to attempt a huge oversized one, cheating and using a bit of wire to tie the ends of the first stem is probably best. Put one hand through the centre of the circle and pull one end through the middle, as if you were tying it into a knot. Pull the ends to tighten the circle. It may have slipped open a bit by now, so be sure to put it back to the size you want. Keep wrapping the thinner end around on itself so that the circle starts to hold itself together. If you find the circle keeps popping open, you may have to go a bit smaller. The cut end is often too stiff to wrap around in the same way, so let it stick out a bit. It may mean that the wreath isn't perfectly circular, but don't worry, they always look wonky to start with.

» The most important bit about putting the second stem in (and every next stem) is to make sure that the line of the weaving is going in the same direction. Poke the thickest bit of the stem through the centre of the wreath, check it is going the same way as the end of the last one, and then start to pull the thinner end round and through, round and through. The willow should start to fit into its own groove, like the fibres that make up a rope. It will look a bit uneven for a while and then suddenly come together.

» Trim off any blunt, thick ends that are still sticking out at the end. Decorate with ribbon. Velvet always looks good.

foraging

Oh, it sounds so glorious and free. And it is. There is nothing more exhilarating than coming across the perfect wonky branch, or a holly tree laden with berries, or a clump of mistletoe that has obligingly fallen out of its tree in mid-December. But there are a couple of things you need to know about foraging. You know all those pictures of people in expensive magazines and on Instagram walking through their magnificent front door with swags of rose hips? They're probably photographed in September at the latest. Lots and lots of the things we think we can forage around Christmas time are long gone by then. Either they have fallen from the plant, or been eaten, or are just so over that you probably wouldn't want to decorate your home with them anyway.

The track to my field is lined with old man's beard. A parallel line of clouds and clouds of wild clematis. Sometimes the local farmer obliterates it in mid-September (the track also lines the back of the churchyard) and sometimes I manage to keep a hold of it until the end of October. But by the time I want it for wild and reckless home decorating in mid-December, the seed heads are barely wisps on the wind. They have done what nature intended them to do, which is disperse. There's only so much hairspray can do to hold back the progress of time, although it will keep the seed heads intact on old man's beard for a week or so. Do not feel like you have to try to swim against the tide on this one; you won't win, and you can spend a miserable November stressfully monitoring potential foraging hot spots and then be disappointed.

A lot of the berries you see are likely to be imported or plastic, and if you don't want to use either of those in your Christmas decorations, there are other options. Namely, evergreen foliage and dried materials.

A note on preserving. I can cut a flower or seed head and hang it upside down with the best of them. Once you get into silica and microwaves though, I think it detracts from the natural beauty of the material. The one exception is beech leaves. For beautiful brown leaves you need to (rather counterintuitively) cut them while fully green and put them in a jar of one-part glycerine to two-parts hot water. As the branch takes the glycerine up into the leaves, they gradually change colour. Once fully brown, the branch is ready to be removed. This usually takes a day or so, but it very much depends on how fast your branch is taking up the liquid. If you leave them in too long, the glycerine starts oozing out, so keep an eye on them.

The second thing to remember about foraging is that lots of people are going to be doing it, or wanting to be doing it. Unless you live on your own estate, you need to get permission from the landowner to cut branches or foliage. I am not bold enough to knock on strangers' doors and ask if they would miss a few heads off their pampas grass, as many florists did when hanging grass clouds became so popular. But if you live in an area where people have well stocked and interesting gardens, it is worth steeling yourself to do so – or finding a more confident and brass-necked friend to do it for you.

The sorts of things you are looking for for wreaths are eye-catching, interesting evergreens. Some texture, but not too prickly. I pass a juniper bush most days and there is a conifer at The Old Mill in the village with the most exquisite silvery tips that I have been known to raid (with consent) for a cool Christmas palette. Scots pine gives a softness and a bit of floppiness to your wreath, so embrace the wildness. These are not your shop-bought neat. That said, when you pick up your Christmas tree, ask for some offcuts; these are absolutely perfect for adding bulk and texture.

coming full circle

The size of your wreath depends upon the size (and to some extent the grandeur) of your door. You can have an opulent, generous wreath on a quite small frame – don't think you always need to use a big frame to get drama. If your frame is too big, it'll just look out of proportion and you'll curse it every time you try to go in and out of the house with the shopping. Most doors look absolutely perfect with a 25cm (10-inch) frame. Only barns and Georgian double doors need bigger than that.

Fat wreaths come from big bundles squished close together, not from bigger frames. To that end, you will probably need more foliage than you initially expected. Adding twigs, seed heads and trailing bits will not only help with bulk, it will also give lots of texture and a sense of abundance and of bringing the wild wood in.

A word on sustainability. If you have moss in your lawn, feel free to rake it up, but I try to avoid buying moss in bulk. It is a precious natural resource and I am somewhat suspicious of its sources. A local, sustainable alternative is hay. Easily sourced from a local farmer in the country, or from a pet shop in the town. Give your wreath a soak once it is complete and the hay will hold enough moisture to keep your display looking good for a while.

The general principle is that evergreens like being cool and moist and outside and so are best placed on the front door, especially if you have an open fire or central heating. Dried wreaths or anything fragile will last better indoors, protected from the elements.

an evergreen wreath

YOU WILL NEED
» **25cm (10 inch) copper base ring**

» **Hay or sustainably sourced moss**

» **A ball of string or reel wire**

» **A small bundle of foliage, evergreen or dried twigs, fruits, seedheads**

» **1.5m (5ft) ribbon**

» **Strong secateurs**

» Secure the end of your wire reel or ball of string at a point on the frame. Doing so on a join means it won't slip round so much. Put handfuls of dry hay into the wreath and wrap the wire or string around and around so you have a fat, even sausage. Make the sausage fatter for a bushier wreath, a bit thinner for elegance. Either way, it is the evenness that matters. Put the frame to one side.

» Cut the foliage into lengths. The tips are always easier to make look good, so be creative with the other bits, they might need to be tucked behind other things.

» Make some fan-shaped bundles. Place one big piece at the back and then layer a few other bits on top. Tie at the base of the fan and put the bundle to one side. Repeat. How many of these bundles you need will depend on how lush you want your wreath to be and how big the frame is. It is better to do a few extra at this stage, so err on the side of generous. Maybe 20 at least. They don't all have to be the same in terms of what is in them – indeed, variety will make the wreath look less shop-bought. But they do need to be roughly equal in size and bulk.

» Tie the wire on to the frame again, underneath the hay. Put the first bundle flat on the hay, and wrap the wire around both the bundle and the frame a few times quite tightly. This will stop the bundle rolling backwards and forwards into the centre or towards the outside.

» Without cutting the wire, put the next bundle on top of the first, so the fronds of it cover the stalks. If you are going for elegant, just put it so the fronds only just cover the stalks and the hay cannot be seen. I do think this is harder to make look good, though, so it is not a technique for trying on your first wreath. If you want to hide a multitude of wreathing sins, put the bundles really close together. Wrap the wire around the stems and the wreath again. Wrap it a few times to ensure it is firmly anchored.

» Without cutting the wire, just keep going round the hay base, making sure you are always putting the bundles on in the same direction, always with the fronds covering the stalks of the one before. Every so often check that you are placing them evenly. Don't be tempted to skimp if you think you are going to run out of bundles – just tie off the wire, put the wreath down, and make a few more.

» The last bundle is always tricky and requires a bit of tucking in. Again, do the best you can and mentally mark this bit as the ribbon hanging point.

» You are almost certainly going to make your wreath flat on a table. It will look gorgeous. Perfect. Pert. Lush. But as soon as you finish and hold it up at arm's length to admire, bits of it will move. Pieces of hay that you couldn't see when it was lying flat will suddenly appear. You will realize that one half is fatter than the other. At least one bundle will twist alarmingly. Unless you are a professional and you make a hundred wreaths every Christmas, this is entirely normal. First of all, find the heaviest point of the wreath, where it seems out of proportion and thickest. Twist the wreath so that this is at the bottom. Suddenly, it will look fine. With this at the bottom, tie string or wire at the top and hang it up somewhere. This doesn't have to be its final place, you just need to be able to see what happens when gravity is in play.

» Adjust the bundles a bit so they are more even. Even if you have tied the wire tight, they should move and slide a little bit. Tuck in spare bits of foliage you might have left over from bundle-making to cover any thinner bits, or any hay that is showing. Remember to take a step back and look at it from a distance. Or make a cup of tea and then come back to it. Better still, take a photograph on your phone and then look at the photo. The human eye is so incredibly forgiving and it fills in the gaps and evens out the smooth bits. I cannot tell you how often I have only noticed a gaping hole in a garden, a flower arrangement or a wreath when I have looked at a photo of it.

» Come back to it. Tuck a few more bits in. And a few more for good measure – Christmas is no time for polite tidiness. When you are happy with it, dip the base in some water and let the hay soak it up. Leave it on a draining board for a little while afterwards so the excess water can run off, especially if you have wooden doors. (If you have particularly special doors, you can cut up a plastic bag and pin it on to the back of the wreath to make sure the damp hay does not come into contact with the wood.) Tie on ribbon.

» Hang at eye level.

the five-minute wreath

» **A base**

» **A small bundle
of foliage, either
dried or evergreen**

» **1.5m (5ft) of
mixed ribbons**

» **Florist's snips
or scissors**

At the beginning of Christmas, we are all full of good intentions. All
the mood boards and all the glossy magazines and all your high hopes of
a Christmas so tasteful that it is almost offensive. However, as things go on,
and time runs out, and to-do lists are long, real life can get in the way of
opulent wreaths. This is the one you need when you have about five minutes
between putting the potatoes in the oven and your visitors arriving.

» Find a base for your wreath. This could be a fine brass wire wreath, a rough
vine base (akebia, or chocolate vine, works wonderfully) or, at a desperate
push, an old wire coat hanger.

» Pick a point in the wreath as a focal point, asymmetrical works better –
think 5pm rather than 6pm on the clock face. Wire the foliage at this point.
Because the ring is quite thin and possibly slippery, you need to make sure
you wire it on tight and in more than one place – once at the base and then
again a bit further up. If you have any sticky floral tape, this might help, but
it is fiddly, so I tend to stick to wire and just make sure I wrap it tight and
a few times round.

» Taking the focal point, put another piece of foliage going the other way.
This generally creates a messy meeting point where you can see the cut ends.
A pine cone can hide a multitude of sins, but they also have a tendency to
twist round if they are not really securely attached with wire. Ribbon will
always save the day, though. Just wrap the touching ends with a bit of
velvet and let some trails add a bit of drama.

» Hang it up. Have a mince pie. You're done.

» If you genuinely don't have time even for this, a hanging branch might fit the bill. One attractively shaped bough and something to hang it with. It could be fine ribbon, rustic string or fishing wire, depending on your décor. Tie at each end and hang from a hook. It will probably want to twist around the tying points, so make sure it sits flat against the wall.

boxing day

There has been a change in how I feel about the twelve days of Christmas. The excitement and anticipation, the approaching crescendo quality of Christmas Eve no longer holds the same charm. It is the Boxing Day peace that calls to me now. The rest. The quiet. It is the perfect pause in the heart of the winter, a missed beat of activity, when it is possible to just sit. The season stretches behind, and it is too soon for the flurry and rush of the new year. There is nothing to be done.

I spend the days watching the drips off the thatch. The soil is too wet even for a little hoeing, although this winter has been so mild that the weeds are still coming, and the grass is still growing. (It continues to grow if the temperature is above 7°C (45°F). I cut branches of early catkins from the hazel hedge, and there are signs of growth. Even now, in the quietest times, there are changes in the garden and in the fields. In such a blanket of grey, cloudy hibernation, these changes are even more magical, more noticeable. Freckles, the winter clematis, blooms generously against the wall of the back kitchen. It is still young, not yet tall, each flower hanging bell-like downwards, so I cut the vines of flowers to put them on the kitchen table and see the intricate pattern inside.

This is also a time to raise my eyes to the landscape beyond the garden. The hill on the other side of the valley remains misty for much of the day. We walk along the base of the hills to Netherclay, so called because the soil is so yellow and heavy there you could fashion it into a teacup. Noticing the flow of water in the earth around my garden, how the soil changes in the miles around it, makes me feel like I know my own ground better, its context and its ancestry. It may look like loam, but its deep roots are clay and I must respect that. I must not work it when wet, dig it or deplete it, and in return it will give me the most glorious roses, prolific crab apples, and strong-stemmed cutting flowers.

For now, I must rest.
I must wait.

jobs for winter

ORDER SEEDS FOR NEXT SEASON

SOW SWEET PEAS

CUT BRANCHES AND BRING INTO THE HOME

MAKE A WREATH FOR THE DOOR OR WALL, OR BOTH

resources

SEEDS

My full range of cut flower, sweet pea and kitchen garden seeds are available to subscribers of Gather with Grace Alexander, my monthly membership programme for garden writing, images and films. If you are not a subscriber, many of my seeds can be found at The Future Kept, thefuturekept.com, or see my website, gracealexanderflowers. co.uk, for stockists.

If I source seeds elsewhere, I make sure I choose open pollinated and organic.

SEEDS
Seed cooperative
seedcooperative.org.uk

Tamar organics
tamarorganics.co.uk

Vital seeds
vitalseeds.co.uk

Beans and herbs
beansandherbs.co.uk

For a wider range of cutting garden varieties, try:

Jelitto
jelitto.com
Chiltern seeds
chilternseeds.co.uk

Sweet pea specialists:
English Sweet Peas
englishsweetpeas.co.uk

BULBS
Jacques Armand
jacquesamandintl.com

Peter Nyssen
peternyssen.com

COMPOST
Fertile Fibre
fertilefibre.com

Dalefoot compost
dalefootcomposts.co.uk

VESSELS
Vervain shop
vervainfloraldesign.com

Also check your local reclamation yard and charity shops

TOOLS
Snips, secateurs and pin frogs
Niwaki
niwaki.com

Copper tools
implementations.co.uk

TABLEWARE
Ali Herbert Ceramics
aliherbert.com

Kneeboneware
kneeboneware.co.uk

Rebecca Proctor
rebeccaproctor.co.uk

Sarah Gee Ceramics
sarahgeeceramics.com

RIBBONS
The Natural Dyeworks
thenaturaldyeworks.com

TEXTILES
Merchant and mills
merchantandmills.com

Bailey's Home
baileyshome.com

RECOMMENDATIONS
FOR THE STATES

SEEDS
Ardelia Farm
ardeliafarm.com

Floret
floretflowers.com

Grand Prismatic Seed
grandprismaticseed.com

John Scheeper's Bulbs
johnscheepers.com

Uprising seeds
uprisingorganics.com

Wild Garden Seed
wildgardenseed.com

RIBBONS
Silk and Willow
silkandwillow.com

TEXTILES
Maiwa
maiwa.com

index

about the author

Long before I was a florist, I was a psychologist. I still am. A proper coal face, child protection psychologist. Life is difficult, complicated and often just a bit too intangible for comfort. In 2013, I knew I needed to ground myself. I wanted to stand on the earth, and soil and grass between my toes. I wanted real, touchable, physical beauty. So I got dogs. So I grew flowers. So the seed that became Grace Alexander Flowers was sown.

I grow using biodynamic principles and practices and am now in the transition phase for organic certification. The decision and my commitment to follow this path emerges out of a love for my garden, my countryside and my ground and a respect for the life that shares my field with me. The sowing of a seed is a primitive and primal joy. Putting a plant in the ground and expecting to be there when it bloomed, fruited or swelled was a turning point in human evolution, and the start of home. My flower field and my home are one, and I belong with them.

I have a greenhouse but I grow without polytunnels or artificial heat. When the flowers are ready, they flower. That's their thing. I weed them, water them, and make the most of their beauty. That's mine. I am as guilty as the rest of us of thinking I am separate from nature and that it exists for me to exploit and consume me; I use writing, photography and film-making to remind me to be in the moment, to observe, to appreciate and to be amongst beauty without judgement.

acknowledgements

Firstly, to my husband. Who digs deep and builds strong. We created this magical place together.

To my people, the supporters of my business, sowers of my seeds, the readers of my newsletters and, most of all, the members of Gather with Grace Alexander. Your generosity and kindness seem to have no limit. I would not be the writer I am without your patience and your belief and this book is for you.

To Dean Hearne, who saw potential in me and mine, and who started this book in motion. Without your experience and belief, I would not have been able to go through the process of creating a book. Without your glorious photography, I wouldn't have wanted to. To Jeska Hearne, a source of such wisdom and kindness, for the styling.

To Rob MacKenzie for the map of my world. You and Syreeta have been an inspiration and a source of delight for some time and I could not have been more honoured that you would visit the field and draw it so exquisitely. I will always treasure what you created.

To Harriet and Claire at Quadrille, for your vision, patience and your attention to detail.

The British flowers movement is a growing and expanding one. A movement driven by a group of people (mostly women) who are forging paths in flower growing and the floricultural industry that has very little to do with mass production, air freight, long supply chains, or identical blooms that characterise most of the flowers that can be found in supermarkets, wholesalers and hotel lobbies up and down the country. These are women who are living and selling within their local communities. They are brave, innovative, indomitable women who use creativity and graft to produce a truly ethical and beautiful alternative to commercially produced flowers. Often this is whilst raising children, caring for others or, like me, alongside other careers and jobs. I could not be more proud to be part of this movement and to be supported and inspired by such people. There are too many to mention, but special thanks must go to India Hurst of Vervain, Sarah Statham of Simply by Arrangement, Kelly Chevin, and the Garden Gate Flower Company, who changed my life with one photograph.

To Charles Dowding for having the courage to change the world and the tenacity to keep going. You have not only changed how I think about soil and how I grow, but also showed me what can happen if one holds fast to one's convictions of what is good and what is right.

And to my mother, who made me grow up believing that the first thing you do on arriving absolutely anywhere is to 'go round the garden'.

Publishing Director Sarah Lavelle
Senior Commissioning Editor
  Harriet Butt
Design and Art Direction
  Claire Rochford
Photographer Dean Hearne
Stylist Jeska Hearne
Illustrator Rob Mackenzie
Head of Production Stephen Lang
Production Controller
  Katie Jarvis

Published in 2021 by Quadrille,
an imprint of Hardie Grant Publishing

Quadrille
52–54 Southwark Street
London SE1 1UN
quadrille.com

Cataloguing in Publication Data:
a catalogue record for this book is
available from the British Library.

Text © Grace Alexander 2021
Photography © Dean Hearne 2021
Illustrations © Rob Mackenzie 2021
Design © Quadrille 2021

ISBN 978 1 78713 584 0
Printed in China